THE CUBE TEAPOT

New supplies for the Queen Mary. (University of Liverpool)

THE CUBE TEAPOT

ANNE ANDERSON

edited by Paul Atterbury

RICHARD DENNIS
1999

ACKNOWLEDGEMENTS

I should like to thank the following for their help in the preparation of this book: Paul Atterbury, Maureen Batkin, Peter Boyd Smith of Cobwebbs, Southampton, Hilary Calvert, Sue Chester, Richard Dennis, Malcolm Elliott of the Victorian Society, Leicester Group, Paul Gibbs, Patrick Going, Maria Hallet, Duane Kahlhamer, Peter and Pam Laister, William Miller, Mr Odom, who supplied the photographs of the Crawford family, Jonathan Quayle, Lloyd Rust, Angela Salter, John and Jackie Stream, Roger Vercoe, and Wendy Wort. My warm thanks to Sue Evans for her many hours of painstaking work.

My thanks to Leicester Museums Service: Jane May; The Living History Unit, Leicester: Angela Cutting; The Potteries Museum, Stoke-on-Trent: Miranda Goodby and Deborah Skinner; Royal Doulton: Joan Jones; Southampton Cultural Services: Alistair Arnott and Rachael Wragg; Spode: Pam Woolliscroft.

Photographic credits: Cobwebbs of Southampton; Liverpool University Special Collection; London Metropolitan Archives; Southampton Cultural Services; *Tableware International (The Pottery Gazette and Glass Trade Review)*; The Laister Collection; The Potteries Museum, Stoke-on-Trent.

Particular thanks to the Southampton Institute who assisted with reproduction fees!

Above all, I am grateful to Mrs Kemp, Percy Aspinall's daughter, who generously made available to me all the CUBE promotional material in her collection, without which I simply could not have written this book. I met Mrs Kemp through the auspices of the Living History Unit, Leicester, and I dedicate this book to her.

Teapot photography by Magnus Dennis

Print, design and reproduction by Flaydemouse, Yeovil, Somerset

Published by Richard Dennis, The Old Chapel, Shepton Beauchamp, Somerset TA19 OLE, England

© 1999 Richard Dennis & Anne Anderson

ISBN 0 903685 76 0

All rights reserved

British Library Cataloguing-in-Publication Data. A catalogue record for this book is available from the British Library

Sally Tuffin, wife of publisher Richard Dennis, using a CUBE teapot at summer camp, c1946.

CONTENTS

An advertisement for CUBE teaware from 1930. Also used on promotional leaflets.

INTRODUCTION

The story of the CUBE teapot illustrates both British inventiveness and the national obsession with 'improving' things. It reflects the continuing search for the perfect teapot – one which makes a great cup of tea but also does not drip, is easy to pour and can be used and stored away without fear of chipping the spout. Most of the improvers have, over the years, settled for tackling just one of these problems: an infuser for just the right brew, a non-drip or an unchippable spout, or a lock-lid. The CUBE claimed to have combined all these individual needs in one 'perfect' design.

The story of the CUBE, which was to become the world's largest selling patented teapot, goes back to 1917 and yet this famous cubic teapot was still in use on the *QE2* as late as the 1980s. It could be found gracing the tables of Lyons Corner Houses, surviving the open seas on the *Aquitania* and in daily use in homes the length and breadth of the country. It was an inexpensive, ordinary, everyday object, something which few people paid attention to and even fewer are likely to remember. Very common in its day, the CUBE was designed to be used. When broken or chipped it was simply discarded. Eventually it was superseded by new designs in the 1950s and 1960s and, consequently, has acquired both the rarity and the period appeal that often makes a utilitarian object collectable. The CUBE was a novel design, very much a product of the thinking of the day, combining a stylish form with practical features. It was modern but not so ultra-modern that people were deterred from using it. It was produced by many manufacturers, under licence, which means that there are many different makes and patterns to acquire. Today it is very much linked with the inter-war years, with Art Deco and the *moderne* style and especially with the glamour of transatlantic travel for, from 1936, the CUBE was the standard teaware employed on the Cunard *Queens*. The stylish innovations of the 1920s and 30s – angular shapes, bold patterns and bright colours – have caught the public imagination today and so it was only a matter of time before attention was drawn to the CUBE, a teapot so original that it quickly captured a commercial market and inspired many imitators.

However, the story of the CUBE teapot is much more than just the identification of a new collectable. It represents a slice of social history, which includes the CUBE's immediate precursors and its numerous rivals. For this reason this book charts not only the evolution of the CUBE teapot, but also records the other rivals and patented designs such as the NEVVA-DRIP teapot and the CAMEL 'drip-catcher' spout, objects whose utilitarian qualities still appeal more to the historian than the collector.

The CUBE belongs to a period in history when stopping for a cup of tea in the afternoon was the norm. The latest statistics show that for the first time the consumption of coffee has now overtaken tea, but before the Second World War, it was tea in the morning, even before rising, tea for 'elevenses', and tea at 4 pm precisely. As the song declared, 'Everything Stops for Tea'. Tearooms were everywhere, especially in non-conformist cities where abstinence was encouraged. The Tea and Coffee Shop Movement, as it has been called, was in part inspired by the campaign to encourage alternatives to hard drink and partly by the new requirements of shopping. Unlike their male counterparts, ladies 'up to town' for the day did not have a club to which they could go, and they certainly could not take refreshments in a public house. They needed a proper environment for a rest and a drink – a place in which to meet friends and socialise. In cities such as Glasgow and Leicester tearooms abounded, offering a wide range of social services from reading rooms and billiard rooms to *de luxe* surroundings for luncheon. Most department stores had a tearoom, and teawares were needed that were stylish, practical and cheap.

According to Margaret Allan, writing in *Good Housekeeping* in 1926, running a tearoom appealed to many ladies who were 'obliged to earn their own living'. If done properly, it could be both lucrative and enjoyable. First and foremost, she suggested, the general atmosphere of the tearoom should be bright and pleasing. If the room was of the 'olde-worlde' variety, quaint patterned curtains and cottage pottery would look delightful with old Windsor chairs and dark oak beams. It was important to reduce costs such as laundry bills – according to *The Pottery Gazette* in September 1920, 'There is nothing more annoying to a purchaser than a teapot that drips, soiling the tablecloth every time it is used.' This was

Changing fashions throughout the years: the famous Lyons' 'Nippies', from the 1890s to the 1930s. (London Metropolitan Archives)

Lyons' advertisement showing their Strand Corner House, 1947. (London Metropolitan Archives)

obviously a problem of some magnitude, featuring in a short story *Christopher and Columbus*, published in 1912. The hero, Mr 'Teapot' Twist, after considerable intellectual effort evolved a successful non-trickler teapot. Small wonder that so many manufacturers devoted their efforts to perfecting the 'non-drip' spout. The CAMEL teapot, for instance, promised to pay for itself in a few months by the savings in laundry bills! According to Margaret Allan, it was vital that serviceable crockery should be purchased that could be replaced individually as there were bound to be breakages. With the proper backing of initiative, tact and common sense, running a tearoom was an ideal occupation, but one had to remember that from the time the door was open until the shutters went up, it was necessary to be ever ready to attend to the wants and comfort of customers.

Although there were many independent tearooms, the teashop boom was really precipitated by chains such as Lyons. There were essentially two types of catering, temperance and commercial. Temperance public houses aimed to create an environment in which people could enjoy all the comfort, warmth and social life which they sought in a traditional public house while drinking tea and coffee rather than beer and spirits. By 1879 there were 100 such establishments in London alone. Five years later there were 232 limited liability companies owning 667 coffee houses with an additional 646 independent institutions. In the 1880s many of these found themselves in financial trouble, partly due to inefficiency and general incompetence. It had also been wrong to assume that working men only went to public houses for the social life. Coffee was no substitute for beer! Consequently many such establishments redirected their activities by offering food, entertainment or by raising prices to attract a better clientele. Gradually the Temperance Movement evolved into an industry as it became clear that philanthropy without commercial success was not viable. Cafes had to be self-supporting, even if they were designed to keep the working man from the evils of drink. In effect, there was little to distinguish these reforming societies from catering firms providing light refreshments with no other motive than to make a profit.

By the 1890s catering companies offered respectable premises, noted for cleanliness and hygiene, to the traveller up from the country, as well as the town dweller. Among those who responded to this new taste for tearooms was Montague Gluckstein, whose background was in the tobacco trade, and his partner Joseph Lyons, who began their catering career with contract catering for exhibitions. Their first major breakthrough was in 1887 when they secured the catering contract for the Newcastle Exhibition. Founding a chain of teashops represented a large investment but this seems to have been the intention from the opening of the first teashop in Piccadilly, London, in 1894. The basic idea was to provide uniform prices within standardised surroundings. The first teashop had a white and gold fascia, which was replicated all over the country, with red silk-covered walls, and gas-lit chandeliers hung from the ceiling. Plush red chairs completed the opulent effect. Smart waitresses in a grey uniform with voluminous skirts down to the floor, served the customers. The menu was light and sophisticated in its range and combined with superior decoration was to appeal to ladies out shopping, to clerks who returned home for a hot evening meal and, above all, at the turn of the century, to the growing army of London typists. Two years later there were seventeen teashops which, by 1939, had grown into 200 teashops in London and 50 in the provinces. However, Lyons still offered a cup of tea of the highest quality and 'still made in an earthenware teapot'. Respectability, quality, cheapness, speed and cleanliness became the Lyons watchwords, based on a small profit on a large turnover. The company boasted of the 'Excellence of a cup of tea and its modest price'.

The famous restaurants also began to appear during the 1890s with the Trocadero in Piccadilly, opening in 1896. This was to become the 'centre of pleasure seeking London', as dining out became respectable for wives and families. However, single ladies were discouraged! Lyons benefited from the general improvement in standards of living and the increasingly large numbers of people forced to spend long periods away from home. Between 1895 and 1914 a new teashop was opened on average every six weeks. The first London Corner House, Piccadilly, opened in 1909 and was followed by the Strand in 1915 and Oxford Street and Marble Arch after the war. They provided anything from a snack to a five-course meal. These were enormous establishments, providing seating for 1,500 to 3,000 people. The Corner Houses became known as the Four Corners of London. They provided music, thick-pile carpets and an atmosphere of luxury but at modest prices.

Lyons was not without rivals. Peace and Plenty operated the British Tea Table, while Lockharts ran the Ideal Restaurants which also catered for the middle-class teashop trade. However, during the interwar years, Lyons emerged as the country's largest caterer. By that time they were operating 250 teashops, three Corner Houses, each seating up to 3,000 people and their flagship, the Trocadero. Between 1900 and 1959, 84 teashops were opened in the provinces and the company employed 22,000 staff. Lyons waitresses, the famous 'Nippies', were accepted as 'the symbol of public service' and the company created a nationally recognised slogan, 'Where's George? Gone to Lyonch!'

Lyons fed the nation at the Empire Exhibition of 1924 – their success based on good value, created by offering popular prices at good trading sites. During the 1930s the company became less profitable, a shorter working week and 'tea in the office' clearly having an effect. In 1957, Lyons teashops still served three million people a week and were also supplying 150,000 retailers with tea, cornering some fifteen percent of the national market. The company sold tea extensively abroad in Canada, South Africa, Rhodesia and Ireland. Through their subsidiary, Hornimans, they supplied 60 countries. Tea drinking was a major part of the Lyons business empire. However, in 1981 the last of the 351 original Lyons white and gold teashops closed. Habits have changed. We may drink more coffee than tea now but we still enjoy stopping in a café for a drink and a chat. Indeed, the café-pub seems to be the phenomenon of the late 1990s, suggesting that the modern consumer enjoys the sociability of such establishments, as well as the chance to drink!

During the age of the tearoom the CUBE teapot owed its success to its compact design and commercial practicality. The CUBE was a product of its day, a reflection of the popularity of taking tea in style in a Lyons Corner House or on the RMS *Queen Mary*.

CREATING THE PERFECT POT

> The day of the traditional teapot – the teapot with the long, inquisitive spout and ungainly handle – is ended. All these years they have gone their way – a sorry succession of chipped and broken vessels. They are out of date and out of favour. The CUBE, once you have made friends with it, is yours for life – too compact to chip and too convenient to discard. It comes to stay. And you cannot invite it too soon. (From a promotional leaflet issued by the CUBE Teapot Co., c1926)

The British obsession with drinking tea, which dates back to the eighteenth century, is well known. Less obvious but equally obsessive is the British compulsion to 'improve' the design of the teapot. This does not only apply to enhancing the flavour of the tea with all manner of ingenious methods of brewing and infusing, but also to improving the durability, safety and pouring abilities of the pot. It seems that the British lady was as concerned with the safety of her teapot lid and the soiling of her pure white tablecloth with ugly drops of tea, as she was with the taste of the tea itself. Also from the early days of the eighteenth century there was a desire for novelty in design which transformed the practical teapot into a collector's item – destined to be looked at, rather than used. This culminated in the 1930s with Sadler's famous teapots in the shape of a motor car or a railway locomotive. One design of 1924 which defies the imagination, was produced especially for the British Empire Exhibition. The teapot cover, protected by patent of course, was decorated in such a way that it was possible to tell the time in any part of the British Empire; so even if the pot dripped, or the handle burnt your knuckles, you were able to tell what time it was in Ontario or Melbourne!

By the end of the nineteenth century the concept of the novelty teapot was well established. The most famous must be the teapot based on Oscar Wilde, produced by Royal Worcester c1882. The Aesthetic Movement elevated the utilitarian teapot to a work of art and the cartoons by Du Maurier, published in *Punch* from the later 1870s, depicted women hugging their teapots as though they were new-born babies. In a well-known send up of aestheticism, the creed of 'art for art's sake', the teapot was singled out as an object of desire:

> Mrs Blyth: I've a beautiful cracked teapot downstairs, which has seen plenty of service. Its best days are in store for it

when it becomes the property of an intense enthusiast – as cracked as itself – who will bestow on it as much care and attention as she would on an aged and valuable relative in her second childhood, and treat it as carefully as a baby after vaccination.

Olive: We may learn much from a teapot – to contemplate the harmony of colour and beauty of form. The nearer to the Great Ideal Perfection it may be the more must we energise to live up to it. (from F.C. Burnand, *The Colonel*, British Library, 1881)

Not only does this illustrate that the teapot had become a fashionable 'collectable' but also that it had been reduced to an object of derision. The cult of the teapot had become an obsession – imagine worrying about living up to one's teapot! In the 1890s there was a backlash against aestheticism, which was seen by many as effeminate and decadent. The antics of the artistic and foppish dandy who worried about his dress and interior decorating, were countered by the new 'health' movement which promoted body building, physical exercise and an outdoor life. Even the teapot was given a radical overhaul, as designers turned to improving its function, concentrating on the tea-making capacities of the teapot rather than its appearance. These improvements largely concerned flavour (infusers), safety (lock-lids), pouring (non-drip spouts) and reduced breakage and storage (concentrating on the reduction of the spout and handle and often specifically designed for the hotel and restaurant trade). However, these features were frequently treated in isolation rather than attempting to create a unified whole. It was not until 1916, with the emergence of the CUBE, that an ambitious design brought an holistic approach to the demands of the teapot.

The CUBE is unique for a variety of reasons, not least because its body is completely cubic with no projecting spout or handle. In terms of precursors one could look to the work of Christopher Dresser, the well-known designer associated with the Aesthetic Movement. Dresser was one of the first to consider together the form and function of the teapot. His intense interest in Japanese art and design led him to develop linear, simplified forms which were both aesthetically pleasing and practical. For a Victorian, Dresser took the radical step of speaking out against excessive ornamentation, asserting that it should be entirely subservient to form and could even be

THE SIX-MARK TEA-POT.

Æsthetic Bridegroom. "IT IS QUITE CONSUMMATE, IS IT NOT?"
Intense Bride. "IT IS, INDEED! OH, ALGERNON, LET US LIVE UP TO IT!"

From Punch, *1881.*

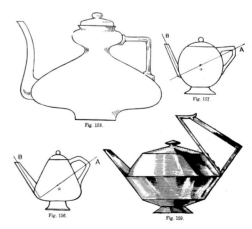

From Principals of Victorian Decorative Design *by Christopher Dresser, 1873.*

omitted! He stated that, 'An object should...be perfectly adapted to meet all the requirements of the work to which it is assigned.'

Dresser's scientific approach and practicality is best illustrated by his analysis of the effects of gravity on the lifting and pouring of the pot, with the handle so placed to minimise the stress on the user's arm. He produced a detailed study of the laws governing the application of handles and spouts. Vessels should be easy to lift and pour well, which Dresser maintained was dependant upon the relationship of the angle of the handle and spout to the centre of gravity. He produced a series of teapots which were radical for their time, the most adventurous being cubic in shape, in which he modified different elements of the design. He did not develop one perfect pot but rather a family of different types. However, this concern with the function and interaction of the various parts of a vessel resulted in an attempt to produce a teapot in which all the elements were integrated. This set in train a long process of development that culminated in the CUBE teapot, the 'climax in teapot construction'.

STRAINERS AND SPOUTS

From the end of the nineteenth century, the teapot manufacturers began to introduce improved forms. Particular attention was paid to the spout, the lid and any vulnerable projections. Normally these improvements concerned one aspect of the teapot, for example, Bailey's PATENT STRAINER teapot of 1898; Green's ACME spout introduced in 1899; the CAMEL drip-less spout which arrived on the scene in 1925; and the HOOK-LID teapot manufactured by Lingard, Webster and Co. of Tunstall from May 1915. These new features were often grafted onto traditional forms, leading to ungainly looking vessels. There was a definite need to improve the teapot's performance: to reduce the soiling of linen, to reduce breakage and improve storage but there was also the commercial pressure to produce modern, fashionable and desirable shapes. Increasing concerns over health and hygiene were also contributory factors in the evolution of the *moderne* style teapot. The new designs were aimed at the commercial world of hotels and restaurants, as well as the domestic sphere.

Several designs tackled infusing, as makers were concerned to:

safeguard your nervous system and digestion by absolutely separating the tea leaves from the water before the injurious element called tannin has had time to do its evil work.

Such were the claims of the S.Y.P., Wedgwood's 'Simple Yet Perfect' teapot, which was tilted on its side until the tea had brewed in a separate compartment and then righted to pour the tea, without any leaves. However, this was not a simple pot to make as ten separate, moulded pieces had to be assembled. It may have made a good cup of tea but it was certainly not a perfect pot which, perhaps, explains why it was only in production from c1901-1912.

Fortunately there were less complicated alternatives, such as Bailey's PATENT STRAINER teapot, which promised no tea leaves in the cup, and the HARROGATE INFUSER, advertised in *The Pottery Gazette* in January 1916. The latter was produced by T.G. Green and Co. at the Church Gresley Potteries, Swadlincote, near Burton-on-Trent. This area had in effect become an annexe of the potteries at Stoke, manufacturing domestic and trade items in bulk. Typically T.G. Green produced dinner, toilet and general earthenware, specialising in teapots including Rockingham, Jet, Samian and Decorated Earthenware. The patented HARROGATE INFUSER teapot was designed so that, 'After the tea has been mashed for five minutes the infuser is raised and rests on the natch of the teapot.' Dexterity was required when pouring!

Green's had been improving the design of their teapots for several years. In 1899 *The Pottery Gazette* made the important announcement that the company had registered a new teapot spout called the ACME. Gracefully moulded, the makers claimed that it was impossible for the tea to dribble down the spout onto the tablecloth. According to the *Gazette*, 'There is nothing more annoying to a purchaser than a teapot that drips...'

Green's ACME spout was adapted to several of their teapot shapes, including the *Ivanhoe* and, despite looking a little clumsy, was still in use in 1922. In that year *The Pottery Gazette* congratulated the company on their invention of a non-drip spout, commenting:

After trying spouts cut at different angles without success, they found that the only effective way of preventing the drip satisfactorily was by having a projection under the spout for

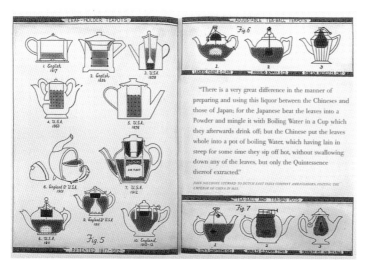

Promotional leaflet issued by Tetley's showing methods of infusing. (LMA)

Advertisement for the Harrogate Infuser, The Pottery Gazette, January 1916.

Advertisement from The Pottery Gazette, May 1898.

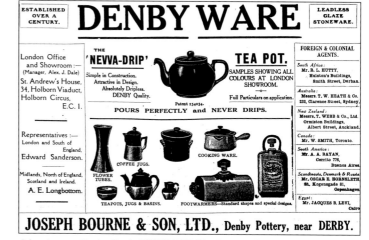

Advertisement for the Denby NEVVA-DRIP, The Pottery Gazette, October 1922.

Right, teapot with Green's ACME spout, illustrated in The Pottery Gazette, April 1922.

Far right, a patent drawing of the PERFECT TEAPOT. The Century Pottery launched their non-drip teapot in 1921.

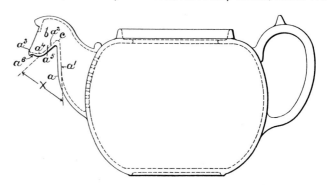

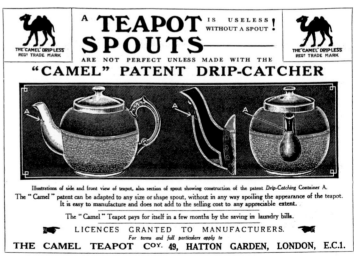
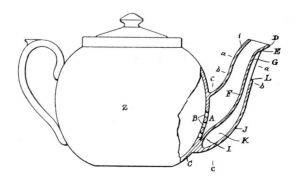

Far left, advertisement from The Pottery Gazette, December 1926.

Left, the CAMEL drip-catcher, Patent No.234698.

Top, advertisement from The Pottery Gazette, July 1927.

Above, advertisement from The Pottery Gazette, July 1926.

the last drop to hang upon, and by having a formation of a bird's throat inside the spout.

Evidently there were some customer doubts, due to the spout's appearance, with potential purchasers 'seeming to think the projection may get knocked off in use' but apparently 'these fears are quite unsubstantiated and in use the non-drip is most clean, as it does not need a teapot stand.' Harrod's Stores retailed these teapots but according to *The Pottery Gazette* sales were small, due to a lack of publicity.

Despite poor sales, Green's non-drip spout aroused interest in the trade with rivals appearing on the scene. In 1921, F. Tunnicliff of The Century Pottery, Burslem (Classic Art Pottery Co.), announced the development of a non-drip teapot (Patent registered October 1921, No.28,401/21; Patent accepted August 1922, No.185,042). For several years this firm had been specialising in lines for the café and restaurant trade, including teapots, coffee pots, hot-water jugs, and butter pats – everything for the caterer with the exception of cups and saucers and plates. These lines were produced in stoneware which is very strong and therefore particularly suitable for such purposes. In order to stimulate demand for their products, the company had been working for some time on the production of an absolutely non-drip teapot and at last they had produced a teapot that they believed to be 'it'. Designed after a scientific study of the mechanism of the flow of liquid from a covered container, the company guaranteed it to be a perfect pourer. According to *The Pottery Gazette* in August 1921, 'It would be too long a process and too abstruse for us to attempt to convey to the reader what the alleged principals are.' However, after testing, the pot appeared to live up to its claims. The teapot was produced in various shapes, with the spout modelled to suit the shape of the pot, but on the same principals, which were claimed to render dripping impossible. Other advantages were a simple and effective self-locking lid; a handle so built into the body as to minimise breakages; a strong, short spout designed especially to reduce breakages and a very flat bottom to give stability. No wonder the pot was named THE PERFECT TEAPOT. Already produced in stoneware, the company hoped to manufacture similar pots in Jet and Rockingham and even in china if there was a demand. The non-dripping, self-locking PERFECT TEAPOT was shown at the British Industries Fair of 1923 by the Classic Art

Pottery Co., with cloisonné decoration along with various styles of chintz patterns and lustre colours. Obviously the firm was going up market! The catering trade were offered more moderately-priced teapots.

The next year Joseph Bourne and Son, also manufacturers of stoneware and the makers of Denby pottery, announced the invention of a non-drip teapot following similar lines, involving a scientifically designed spout. The rapidity with which this company responded to the threat of a new product demonstrates how rival companies needed to maintain their competitive edge, Bourne's aptly christened their new teapot the NEVVA-DRIP (Patent No.154034). This patent drip-less teapot was devised along rather convoluted principals, as reported by *The Pottery Gazette* in February 1922:

> The spout is preferably formed so that the top of the bend is carried very high, as near to the level of the top of the pot as possible, the bend itself being modelled rather sharp, and the passage in the angle nipped in or narrowed to form a bridge-like cut-off. The distance to the outlet of the spout is short, the face of the outlet sloping backwards so as to leave the lower part projecting well beyond the upper.

The result of this was:

> that when the pouring of the tea has finished, and the pot is held in an upright position, any liquid left in the spout either instantly drips into the cup or runs back into the pot.'

Furthermore the design, with the spout above the usual height of the liquid in the pot, also prevented splashing and overflowing as the pot was carried about. Expressed more simply the pot 'claims to be a non-drip and it certainly appears to be living up to what it affects to be.'

Apparently where the new pot scored over others was in its appearance, having the 'merit of being a faultless pourer without being unsightly and, hitherto, the two qualities do not always seem to have run together', perhaps a reference to Green's ACME spout? The company produced an attractive leaflet describing the characteristics of the new pot and made use of promotional incentives such as special showcards and a free tie-on disc to purchasing dealers. More sophisticated marketing techniques were increasingly used to publicise new products, both when they were launched onto the market and to sustain their position. The NEVVA-DRIP was invariably featured in Bourne's advertising in *The Pottery Gazette* and did

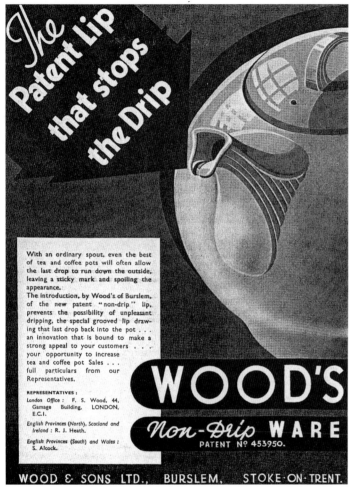

Advertisement from The Pottery Gazette, *August 1938.*

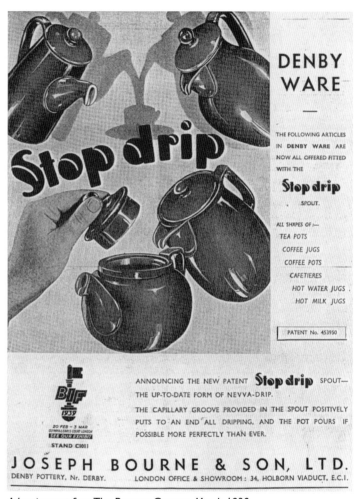

Advertisement from The Pottery Gazette, *March 1939.*

not suffer, as Green's ACME spout, from a lack of publicity. According to the manufacturers the NEVVA-DRIP was, 'Simple in Construction, Attractive in Design, Absolutely Dripless, DENBY quality: Pours Perfectly and Never Drips.' Another advertisement in 1926 proclaimed, 'The Pot That Sells Itself'.

Other non-drip teapots were modelled along the lines of the NEVVA-DRIP. Lovatt and Lovatt made the very similar Langley SAFETY Non-Drip Teapot, advertised in *The Pottery Gazette* in 1927, while the Anchor Pottery came up with the non-chip and non-drip, SAFETY FIRST.

In 1925 the CAMEL drip-catcher spout arrived, which was adapted to different teapot shapes and manufactured by several companies (Patent accepted 1925, No.234, 698, filed by Mr Charles Edward Green, 49 Hatton Garden, London, and Mrs Kathleen Sinclair Stevenson, 40 Queen's Gate Terrace, London). The advertisement in *The Pottery Gazette* in July 1926 claimed that a 'Teapot is useless without a spout', damning its spoutless rivals like the CUBE and HANDY HEXAGON. Evidently the CAMEL teapot paid for itself in a few months by the savings in laundry bills! The CAMEL was in effect an elaborate combined spout and drip-catcher, comprising:

a chamber or receptacle forming part of the spout and into which drips will pass when the pot is stood upright after pouring out some of the contents and be retained instead of the drips falling on to the tablecloth or tray.

A channel carried any residue from the lip into a chamber at the base of the spout and any drips which trickled down 'guide themselves obediently into the channel and not on to the tablecloth.' Unlike other non-drip spouts the CAMEL claimed to be more efficient, to be effective even if the spout was chipped, did not alter the shape of the pot and would not increase the cost to the buyer. Less believable was the assertion that it was easy to clean! Charles Green of Green Bros and Edis, began trading as the CAMEL Teapot Co. in 1926. The enterprising Arthur Wood of Longport, was one of the first to adopt the CAMEL, as advertisements indicate. The spout that spared 'tablecloths and tempers' was licenced to manufacturers including Booth's of Tunstall and Albert Pillivuyt & Co., makers of the famous French fireproof APILCO ware. In 1927 *The Pottery Gazette* commented that Mr Green 'looks forward to the day when his patent will be embodied in all teapots as a matter of course.'

One would have thought that the CAMEL was the last word in non-drip teapots but there was still one major contestant to appear on the scene, 'the Patent Lip that stops the Drip', offered by Wood's of Burslem. A special grooved lip, drawing that last drop back into the pot, was what the housewife needed, according to the advertisement in *The Pottery Gazette* in August 1938. The inventors, Mr and Mrs Arcari of Cremona, had come up with a device that could be fitted to any lip in any material, even glass. In their wisdom the Executive Council of the Institute of Hygiene had granted to Mr and Mrs Arcari their Certificate of Merit and installed representative examples in their Museum of Hygiene. According to them, such a device would be invaluable in the Tropics, as the prevention of soiled tablecloths would reduce contamination from flies! Not to be outdone, Denby responded by updating their NEVVA-DRIP, which was now fitted with the STOP DRIP spout. Its capillary groove 'positively puts to an end all dripping and the pot pours if possible more perfectly than ever', as claimed in *The Pottery Gazette* in March 1939.

THE LOCK-LID

When not concerned with the teapot's pouring abilities, the designer's attention turned to the lid. This was an obvious area of concern, being a matter of safety as well as practicality. The most prominent company in this area was Lingard, Webster and Co. of Tunstall, teapot specialists, whose 'unique' HOOK-LID appeared in May 1915. In fact this was not really a new idea, as late eighteenth-century Castleford-type teapots also featured a safety lid. *The Pottery Gazette*

Advertisement from The Pottery Gazette, *January 1916.*

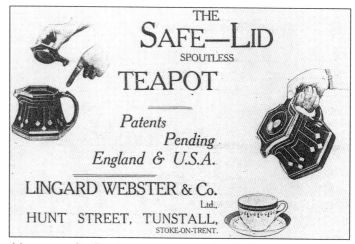

Advertisement from The Pottery Gazette, *October 1923.*

Advertisement from The Pottery Gazette, February 1926.

Robert Crawford Johnson who patented the CUBE teapot in 1917.

referred to the HOOK-LID teapot as 'one of the most successful lines they have ever introduced.' The design was simple and effective, involving a hook at the top of the handle by which the lid was secured through a hole in its rim. In 1923 the company reversed the idea with the SAFE-LID teapot. This had a stopper on a flanged rim which fitted into a hole at the top of the handle. Following the success of the CUBE, the company introduced a hexagonal spoutless teapot fitted with this ingenious mechanism. Not content with these two devices, they then produced the GEM SAFE-LID (Reg No.750,957) in 1932 and the XL (Reg No.808382) in 1936, which also used the idea of a hook. The ingenuity put into such devices defies belief!

THE CUBE

The CUBE teapot attempted to integrate as many of these features as possible into one compact shape. 'A revolution in teapot design', the CUBE has become synonymous with 1930s modernity with its simple, cubic shape and emphasis on safety and hygiene. The 'ultimate in teapot construction' the CUBE's form reduced the spout to little more than an opening in one corner, the handle was recessed into the body and the lock-lid was sunk into the flat top. The cubic form allowed for easy

The Johnson family home, Glen Capel, Central Avenue, Leicester.

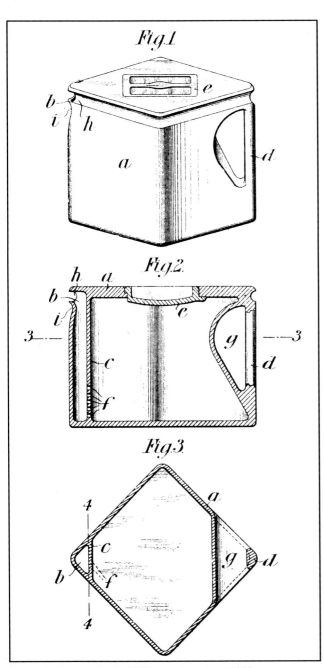

Fig.1

Fig.2

Fig.3

Patent specification for the CUBE teapot, accepted 1917.

110,951

PATENT   SPECIFICATION

Application Date, Nov. 13, 1916.   No. 16,237/16.

Complete Left, May 14, 1917.

Complete Accepted, Nov. 13, 1917.

PROVISIONAL SPECIFICATION.

Improvements in Teapots, Coffee-pots and like Vessels.

I, ROBERT CRAWFORD JOHNSON, of Glen Capel, Central Avenue, Leicester, in the County of Leicester, Managing Director of Robert Johnson & Co. (Leicester) Ltd., do hereby declare the nature of this invention to be as follows:—

My invention relates to teapots, coffee-pots and like vessels.

5   A teapot or the like as now generally constructed is provided with a spout and with a handle projecting from the body and which are liable for this reason, especially in hotels, restaurants and the like, to be injured or broken.

The object of my invention is to obviate this liability and to this end my invention consists in constructing the spout and the handle so that they
10   practically form a part of the body and are thus less liable to be injured or broken than heretofore.

In a pot constructed according to my invention the spout is formed by applying to the inner wall of the body a partition which forms a channel extending from near the bottom of the vessel to a hole or aperture formed near the top
15   thereof, whilst the handle is formed by making a hollow or depression behind a portion of the outer wall, in such a way that the said handle is attached to the wall at the upper or lower ends, whilst openings are formed on either side of the said handle through which the fingers can be passed to grip the handle.

My improved pot can be made of any desirable shape, that is to say, either
20   square, round, oval or otherwise, and ornamented in any desired manner. The first mentioned shape is very advantageous where several pots have to be stored or packed together as they will fit without loss of space; also the top of the pot is advantageously made flat and provided with a lid which is level with or below the top surface so that the pots can stand one upon another.
25   When the square form is used the spout is preferably arranged in one angle of the vessel and the handle is formed at the opposite angle.

It is to be understood that the improved pot can be of moulded earthenware or the like or made of metal.

Dated the 13th day of November, 1916.

30
G. F. REDFERN & Co.,
15, South Street, Finsbury, E.C., and
10, Gray's Inn Place, W.C.,
Agents for the Applicant.

[Price 6d.]

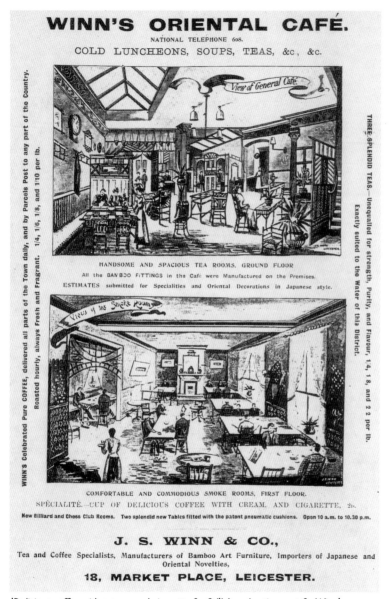

'Delicious coffee with cream, and cigarette for 2d'! An advertisement for Winn's Oriental Café, Leicester, 1910.

The Turkey Café, one of the famous cafés in Leicester, operated by the Winn family, with elaborate Doulton façade by William Neatby, c1900.

stacking both on top and side-by-side. During the 1930s it was produced by the thousands and was used on the great transatlantic liners, on national railways and by major hotels and restaurants. An American style advertising campaign sold the CUBE teapot to the retailer, commercial user and the housewife. The CUBE was manufactured under licence by many different companies including Green, Grimwades, Minton, Sadler, Wedgwood & Co., and Wood.

Although it is thought of as a product of the 1930s, the CUBE teapot was in fact designed before the First World War. Robert Crawford Johnson of Leicester (born 1883) registered his design for a cubic teapot in November 1916 and his application was accepted the following year. The youngest son of Joseph Johnson (1844-1906), who owned and managed the largest and most successful drapery store in Leicestershire, Robert does not appear to have had any formal training in art or design. On the death of his father in 1906 he inherited stock in J. Inglesant and Sons and opened his own business, as a house furnisher and furniture dealer.

Joseph Johnson had started his own business in 1869. This flourished, was enlarged frequently and was housed in splendid premises on Market Street designed by the Leicester architect, Isaac Barradale. Johnson was a Liberal Unionist and nonconformist (his father is thought to have come from a nonconformist background) who attended the Belvoir Street Chapel and was also a Freemason. Johnson's was eventually taken over by Fenwicks in 1962. Joseph Johnson was also chairman of J. Inglesant and Sons Ltd., later taken over by Waring and Gillows. The family lived in Kirby Muxlowe, an exclusive residential area outside the city. The 1891 census listed him as draper, aged forty-seven, along with his wife, Ann (forty-three), daughters Annie (twenty-one), Ellen (eighteen) and sons George (fourteen), Samson (eleven) and Robert C. (eight). According to the terms of Joseph Johnson's will, his daughter Annie received one-third of Joseph Johnson and Co., George Crawford, one-third (he was a managing director by 1905), and one-third went to Margaret Ellsworthy. To Robert, he left all the shares in J. Inglesant and Sons Ltd. Robert Johnson's premises, which expanded rapidly, were at 2, 4 and 6 London Road, Leicester. The Patent Specification gives Robert Crawford Johnson's home as Glen Capel, Central Avenue, Leicester. In *Kelly's Directory* his trade is listed as House Furnishers and Antique Furniture at 2 & 4 London Road, with a depository on Silver Street. By 1925 he was styled Director and had acquired No.6 London Road. His home address was now Roxton, Springfield Road, near London Road, Leicester. The CUBE Teapot Co., Ltd., china dealers, with premises at 157 London Road, is listed in *Kelly's* for 1928. In that year the electoral roll lists Robert Crawford Johnson with Kate Elizabeth Crawford at Springfield Road, Leicester and he can

be traced on the electoral rolls until 1938.

Robert Johnson obviously inherited his father's business acumen but what prompted him to create a cubic teapot is unknown. However, Leicester already enjoyed a progressive reputation in the design world. Harry Peach, founder of the Dryad workshops, was one of the driving forces behind the Design and Industries Association when it was formed in 1915. Dryad secured contracts for the supply of its famous cane furniture to the transatlantic liners, *Aquitania* and *Mauretania*. This furniture was also used in the many tea and coffee houses in Leicester, a city with a long tradition of temperance. Thomas Cook, the famous travel agent, had been one of the leading campaigners in the city against the evils of strong drink. The Turkey Café, of 1900, built by the prominent local architect Arthur Wakerley with a Doulton Carraraware façade, was one of several purpose-built premises, which included a games' room. Another local architect, Edward Burgess, designed the Victoria Coffee House on Granby Street, built in the year of the Queen's Jubilee and opened in 1888. This establishment was built for the Leicester Coffee and Cocoa House Company, a philanthropic organisation which aimed to provide wholesome and non-alcoholic refreshment as an alternative to the intoxicating liquor offered by public houses. The company was established in 1877 by supporters of the Temperance Movement and eight houses were finally opened. According to Robert Read, writing in 1881, the Coffee and Cocoa House Company was 'the most formidable advocate of temperance existing.' All the establishments were airy and bright, offering daily newspapers and other amusements, including billiards, and rooms set aside for women only. Some idea of their size and grandeur can be gleaned from the sale notice of 1922 for the Rutland in Wharf Street: on the ground floor were 39 marble-topped tables on iron frames and over 100 bentwood chairs, plus other seating. The first and second floors contained billiard rooms with eight billiard tables and other accessories. Designed for 'workers of either sex' and to be used from '5 to 9 a.m., 12 to 2 p.m. and again in evening sociability', in practice the larger central establishments tended to attract a wealthier clientele, such as doctors, solicitors and other professional men. To a certain extent these 'grander' establishments, the East Gates and the Victoria, subsidised the other coffee houses which

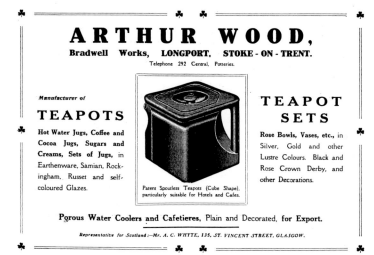

The first advertisement for the CUBE, The Pottery Gazette, October 1920.

suggests that a purely working-class clientele did not generate sufficient profits. The lure of billiard tables and the profit on soup, cocoa, coffee, tea and the unpretentious meals served could not sustain the company. Moreover, the more genteel customers were enticed away by the newer cafés established by Winn's. Although the Coffee and Cocoa House Co. was sold off in 1922, there were plenty of other establishments, including Winn's Turkey Café, Oriental Café, Sunset Café and Café Royal, London Road, on the ground floor of the Wyvern Hotel built for Thomas Cook. Department stores, like Lewis's, whose Leicester branch opened in the 1930s, catered for both the shopper and tea-drinker.

With his business interests, and nonconformist links, Johnson may have been attracted by the commercial potential of a pot with flat surfaces. There was the developing tourist and motoring trade, with the need for portable and durable equipment. CUBE services were fitted into picnic hampers and there was even a camping set! From the outset Johnson was aiming for commercial rather than domestic use:

> A teapot or the like as now generally constructed is provided with a spout and with a handle projecting from the body and which are liable for this reason, especially in hotels, restaurants and the like, to be injured or broken. The object of my invention is to obviate this liability and to this end my invention consists in constructing the spout and the handle

so that they practically form a part of the body and are thus less liable to be injured or broken than heretofore. (Patent Specification 110,951, Application Date 13 Nov, 1916 No. 16,237/16. Accepted 13 Nov, 1917.)

Although any desirable shape could be chosen, square or flat sides and top was the most advantageous, allowing several pots to be stored or packed together, 'as they will fit without loss of space.' The flat top allowed for vertical stacking. Such 'improved pots' could be made of earthenware or metal.

After a delay, presumably because of the war, the CUBE teapot went into production in 1920. Arthur Wood of Longport, Stoke-on-Trent, appears to have been the first to produce an earthenware version. An advertisement in *The Pottery Gazette* of October 1920 records the first appearance of the CUBE teapot, announcing the 'Patent Spoutless Teapots (CUBE Shape), particularly suitable for Hotels and Cafes'. Arthur Wood was a well-known manufacturer of teapots and the April 1921 edition of *The Pottery Gazette* carried a feature on 'Mr Wood's cube-teapot' noting its special features:

> (1) that there is neither handle nor spout to project and (2) that the lid is flush with the top of the pot. This in brief means that the pot will stand anywhere; it is impossible to knock it over; it will stack safely to almost any height; it is easily cleaned, being plain and having an opening as wide as the pot itself; and it will pour perfectly, seeing that the angle of the flow is part of the teapot itself.

Many extravagant claims were to be made about the CUBE's abilities, although many users complained that it dribbled and burnt the knuckles!

After the First World War the manufacturers of commercial tablewares were heavily criticised for their lacklustre revivalist styles. The market was very competitive and makers were looking for designs that were progressive, practical and eye-catching. Arthur Wood tried to stay one jump ahead of his rivals by adopting new designs and innovations as they became available. As *The Pottery Gazette* of July 1926 recorded:

> Mr Wood seems to have always had at the back of his mind the production of special lines in teapots. Hygenic, CUBE and non-drip teapots are lines which are readily associated with his name and factory. Over twenty years ago, Mr Wood had his Hygenic infuser teapot well on the market; it is many years

ago now since he brought out the CUBE teapot and one of his most recent accomplishments has been to adapt the new CAMEL patent dripless spout to a variety of existing shapes.

THE COMPETITION

By this date Arthur Wood was not the sole maker of the CUBE teapot, nor was it the only cubic teapot available. The CUBE had caught on and the number of imitations manufactured by 1925 may be taken as a measure of its success. As early as 1922, Robert Johnson sought legal advice concerning plagiarism and the infringement of his patent. During the 1920s at least eight teapots were produced which attempted to imitate the CUBE which must have been most frustrating for Johnson as he relied on producing the CUBE under licence. Arranged from their date of production they include:

Sadler's HANDY HEXAGON, patented in 1921
Gibson's WEMBLEY, patented in 1922
Abram's COSY, patented in 1922
S. Johnson's GEM, introduced in 1923 with a special non-heating handle
The G.M.C. manufactured by G.M. Creyke & Sons from 1923 with non-breakable spout (it was made of metal!)
The CLIMAX, retailed by Shorter Bros., London, from 1923
The DIAMOND by H.J. Wood, a 'novelty in non-drip pots', introduced in 1924
Lingard. Webster and Co.'s hexagon spoutless teapot with SAFE-LID, 1924
Denby's PEKOE spoutless teapot, specially suitable for restaurant use, was produced alongside their famous NEVVA-DRIP by 1925
Bursley Ltd., Crown Pottery, Bursley Ware SERVICE teapot fitted with a double strainer, almost spoutless and interchangeable lock cover, c1927
Wade, Heath and Co.'s COMPACTO, c1928

The Depression appears to have swept away many of the CUBE's rivals and even Sadler and Gibson were licenced to produce the famous cubic design. Care should be taken not to confuse the CUBE with the teapot used in the Goblin Teasmaid. This electric device for making an early morning cup of tea was not introduced until the mid-1930s. Its cubic-shaped teapot had a hole in the top which took a pipe from the water boiler. When the water reached boiling point it automatically bubbled into the adjoining teapot. At least all the bubbling ensured that one did not go back to sleep!

The CUBE's closest rival was James Sadler's HANDY HEXAGON, patented in 1921. It was probably this model that led Robert Johnson to seek legal advice in January 1922. A document addressed from Mr G.G. Redfern, Chartered Patent Agents, refers to advice about a sample teapot which Johnson regarded as an infringement of his CUBE PATENT (No.110591). A comparison between the original patent specification for Sadler's HANDY HEXAGON and the model that was finally put into production reveals many changes. The final design is much closer to the CUBE and includes a recessed handle, sunken lid and spoutless profile. The HANDY HEXAGON certainly came close to infringing Johnson's patent and yet, evidently, he was unable to take any legal action to prevent the sale of Sadler's teapot or any of the other CUBE lookalikes, which were apparently equally committed to the new philosophy of functionalism and practicality.

James Sadler and Sons, who specialised in teapots, also tried to stay one jump ahead of the competition. Having already introduced the PINE Lock-Lid Teapot (1916) and the NESTA range, a series of nesting pots with sunken lids suitable for the restaurant trade (1920), the company submitted a patent application for a new teapot design in 1921 (PA 22 June 1920 No.16849/20, Accepted 6 Jan 1921, No.156,051). The application was registered by Edward Sadler of Newlands, Watlands Avenue, Wolstanton, Stoke-on-Trent. The illustration shows a rather ungainly shape, which had little bearing on the design that went into commercial production. It has the characteristic indented handle and spoutless profile but it has not yet developed the wide, flat top with sunken lid and it has the addition of a drip-tray under the spout which presumably proved to be impractical. It certainly looks clumsy! Nevertheless, this shape was actually produced, minus the drip-tray, as indicated by *The Pottery and Glass Record* of February 1921. At this stage it had been christened the Handy Shape, Spoutless Teapot. The HANDY Teapot made its debut at the British Industries Fair in February 1921. However, by the following year the design looked very like the CUBE, spoutless, sunken lid and recessed handle but with an hexagonal body. According to the promotional campaign, the HANDY was suitable for

Advertisement from The Pottery Gazette, January 1916, for Sadler's 'PINE' LOCK-LID.

Below, advertisement from The Pottery Gazette, June 1924.

Below right, advertisement from The Pottery Gazette, October 1928.

Advertisement from Cox's Potteries Annual and Glass Year Book, 1923.

Advertisement from The Pottery Gazette, 1924.

Gibson's WEMBLEY teapot. The radical shape was softened by applying traditional patterns, The Pottery Gazette, *September 1924.*

HANDY HEXAGON by James Sadler & Sons Ltd., at the British Industries Fair, 1923.

Series of nesting pots suitable for the restaurant trade, by James Sadler & Sons Ltd., The Pottery Gazette, *April 1920.*

restaurants and hotels and luncheon baskets. Production of the NESTA continued, which had been improved with a corrugated foot and was evidently 'non-splitting and strong'. *The Pottery Gazette* was soon singing the praises of the HANDY HEXAGON, in much the same terms that it had used for the CUBE, adding in November 1922 that:

> The merits of the new pot should have the effect of making it a strong seller, not only for hotel and restaurant purposes, for which it is eminently fitted, but also in the general household trade, where it is equally important that a pot should be not only thoroughly effective in what it purports to do, but safe and economical in use.

Sadler's ran a strong promotional campaign for the HANDY. It was featured in colour on the cover of *The Pottery and Glass Record* in 1926. Advertisements in *Cox's Potteries Annual and Year Book* claimed it was 'The Premier Spoutless Teapot of the Day: Good for Stacking, Better for Packing, Best for Selling' for café, hotel or the home. Available in six sizes, the teapot was offered with a matching jug, sugar, cream and stand. A set was displayed at the British Industries Fair in 1923. In 1926 the 'leading house in teapots' mounted a large display of HANDY teapots at the Fair, which was specially noted by King George and Queen Mary. Evidently the Queen's opinion was 'that it was notably practical'. The HANDY was certainly produced well into the 1930s but after the Second World War, Sadler produced CUBES for the Cunarders.

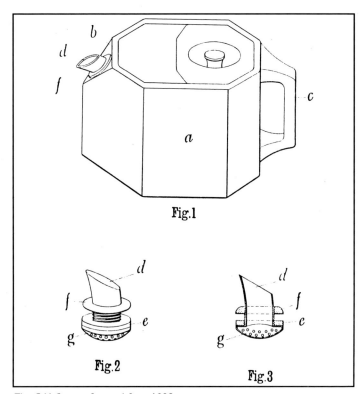

The G.M.C. manufactured from 1923.

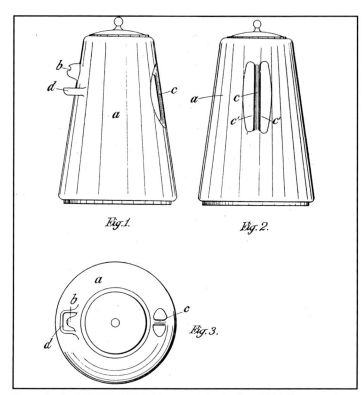

Patent for the HANDY HEXAGON teapot, lodged in June 1920. The original design bears little similarity to the teapot put into mass production.

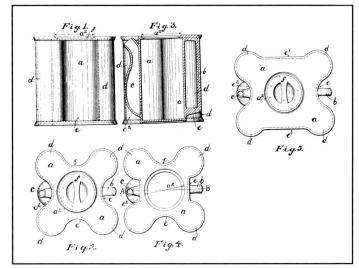

The ingenuity of manufacturers could degenerate into absurdity. This novel design was patented by F. Tunnicliffe of The Century Pottery in 1922.

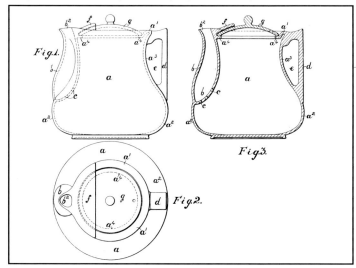

Gibson & Son launched their WEMBLEY teapot in 1922. This is the first version.

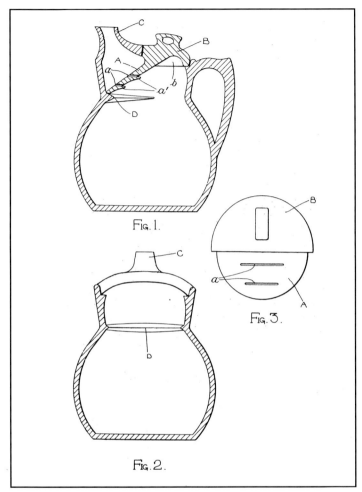

Abram's COSY, patented in 1922.

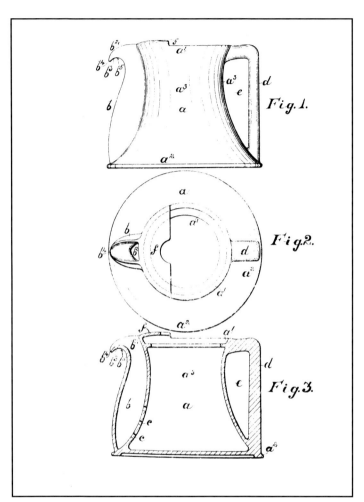

Gibson's modified WEMBLEY, patented in 1923.

Gibson & Sons, who had been teapot specialists for some 50 years, could not afford to lose their premier position in the trade as one of the largest producers. According to *The Pottery Gazette*, Gibson and teapots were synonymous, like Coleman and mustard. Their Albany works was entirely devoted to the production of teapots. Consequently, in November 1920, Arthur Gibson of Albany and Harvey Potteries, Burslem, registered a compact teapot, the WEMBLEY (Patent No.173,128), the object being to reduce the spout and handle to avoid breakage. The tulip shape of this teapot accommodated an integrated spout and a recessed handle,

The DIAMOND shape, produced by H.J. Wood, Regd. No.699084, 1923.

with the additional improvement of a safety-lid held in place by a bridge. Modifications made to the design in 1922 by Sydney Gibson, provided a non-drip spout (Patent No.193,320), which was curved down so that the lip was lower than the underside of the spout The modified WEMBLEY had a more pronounced cubic look and would certainly have given Robert Johnson cause for concern. It was illustrated in a full-page advertisement in *Cox's Potteries Annual and Glass Year Book* of 1923. Gibson claimed that their Patent Safety Teapot was 'Sure to Please'. Evidently in 'great demand', this was the 'Ideal Teapot' for hotels and restaurants, saving up to 75% in breakages. *The Pottery Gazette* carried a feature on Gibson's dripless teapot in September 1924. They commended the new model, which had several creditable features. Both the spout and handle had been reduced but without losing the essential characteristics of a teapot. It could be supplied with a conventional knobbed cover or a sunken lid, for the catering trade. The main virtue of the pot, however, was that it was a perfect pourer:

> We have tested it for ourselves... and we have satisfied ourselves that it is what it is claimed to be – a real non-drip.

Yet by 1925, Gibson was producing the CUBE.

Shorter Brothers of London, established by John Shorter in 1800, were not manufacturers but wholesalers or, more precisely, the proprietors of a large, well-arranged warehouse within two minutes walk of Liverpool Street Station. The firm delivered packed goods in their own petrol and electric lorries within 60 miles of London. Shorter's offered everything from pint mugs and glasses to art candlesticks. By 1923 they were offering the CLIMAX spoutless teapot, but a close look at the patent number, 173,128, reveals that this teapot was none other than the redesigned WEMBLEY as supplied by Gibson. This marketing ploy may have been initiated by Shorter's, who perhaps considered the name WEMBLEY a little boring. The CLIMAX certainly sounds more dramatic, suggesting the apogee of teapot design had at last been achieved.

S. Johnson Ltd., produced a spoutless teapot, the GEM in Rockingham and green glaze, from 1924. According to *The Pottery Gazette*, it had the advantage of being a good pourer; it had a flat lid and therefore stacked well (evidently six high without difficulty); the handle was sufficiently large to permit a good grip and consequently there was no burning of fingers. Lastly, the lid was of a locking type and therefore did not fall off easily. There was practically nothing in the realm of teapots that this firm did not produce, and not only teapots for domestic use, but 'such pots as are specially calculated to meet the needs of caterers.'

Wood and Sons of Burslem, not to be confused with Arthur Wood and Son of Longport, were also involved in the manufacturing of a hygienic teapot, through the Ellgreave Pottery Company with which they were associated. The SERVICE teapot had a short spout which could be easily cleaned. It was made in three sizes with interchangeable covers. Inside there was a lower strainer, as well as one at the spout. Yet 'the shape of the pot does not look eccentric at all.' Wood and Sons also manufactured the COSY pot or the 'world's utility jug', which greatly interested the King and Queen at the British Industries Fair of 1926. Evidently Queen Mary informed her husband that she already possessed one. The jug took its name from its double lid which was said to keep liquids hot for twice as long as an ordinary pot. It also claimed not to drip and that the patent strainer kept back all the 'leaves, grounds or pips'. The strainer was like a removable shutter which formed part of the lid. Although made by Wood and Sons, the COSY was patented by Edmund William Abram in 1921 (Patent No.188,503) and, like the CUBE, was produced under licence from Abram Allware Ltd., of London.

One of the CUBE's better-known rivals was the G.M.C. teapot produced by G.M. Creyke and Son, invented by George Walker Creyke of Stockton Brook, Stoke-on-Trent (Patent No.691, registered 1 July 1922 and accepted 5 July 1923). This company could certainly claim that the spout of their teapot was unchippable and unbreakable – it was metal and the spout was literally screwed in. The teapot's principal feature was this detachable, unbreakable and non-rusting spout, which the makers claimed was not only a perfect pourer but that it was impossible for it to drip. *The Pottery Gazette* in January 1923 considered that such a spout, which was 'unobtrusively contrived that it is not an eyesore', was ideal for hotels, restaurants and liners where many teapots met their doom through a broken spout.

THE CUBE TEAPOTS COMPANY

With so many rivals, the CUBE needed rigorous marketing. This led to the forming of the CUBE Teapots Co., Ltd. of Leicester in c1925. The company, established by Robert Johnson and managed by Percy Aspinall, was solely concerned with the marketing and distribution of the CUBE and associated teawares. A feature appeared in *The Pottery Gazette* on 1 October 1925:

> Cube Teapots Ltd., Campbell Yard, Leicester, as their name implies are solely concerned with the now familiar 'cube' teapots. Many inventions have been brought out in connection with the teapot, but none, surely, has been so revolutionary as the 'cube'. This teapot, the inventors claim, eliminates all the faults of its predecessors, while it adds to itself new and necessary virtues. Although its shape follows that of a cube, it is not so geometrical in design that it loses all vestige of daintiness; in fact, to many, in view of the present desire for simplicity in decoration, its concealed spout, sunken lid and built-in handle give an added charm.

Evidently the distributors were not content to leave the retailer to sell the CUBE teapot to the public without the help of good advertising. They offered a 'splendid range of coloured showcards, two leaflets and a charming booklet, illustrating, in their natural colours, the different designs in which the CUBE is made'. Indeed it appears that the CUBE was backed by a 'lively and aggressive selling organisation'. Perhaps their most ingenious sales-aid was a moving display, demonstrating the 'perfect pouring of the CUBE', by tea perpetually pouring from the teapot into a cup. This was a permanent fixture in the window of the Leicester Showrooms at 157 London Road, but evidently it was also sent out on loan. In addition the CUBE Teapots Co. could supply a:

> series of window displays in different sizes, depicting in a very realistic fashion the old era – a teapot with a broken spout, and stained cloth, etc. – and the new era with the CUBE teapot, an immaculate table, a tidy maid, and a satisfied mistress.

To aid the retailer in his selection of these 'attention arresting helps' the company produced a leaflet. The advertisement that appeared in *The Pottery Gazette* on 1 September 1925, listed the merits of the CUBE teapot:

The CUBE Teapots Co. at the Nation's Food Exhibition, 1925.

From *The Pottery and Glass Record, 1925.*

Advertisement from The Pottery Gazette, September 1925. Note the list of manufacturers of the CUBE.

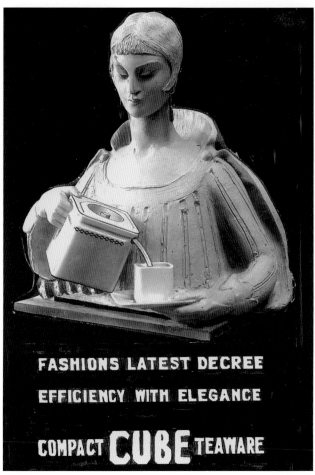

This stylish lady perpetually poured tea in the window of the CUBE Teapots Co's showrooms at 157 London Road, Leicester.

Evolution! The CUBE Teapot.
Here at last is the Teapot you have waiting for and wanting badly.
The square compact shape. The dainty design. The concealed spout. The built-in handle. The sunken lid. The strainer.
All combine to make the CUBE the essence of efficiency-relegating to the scrap heap for evermore the shapeless old-fashioned 'has-been'.
The Brilliant Climax in Teapot Construction.

The same advertisement listed those potters manufacturing the CUBE under licence:

E. Brain & Co., Ltd. Foley China
Wedgwood & Co.
George Clews & Co., Brownhills Pottery
Arthur Wood
Gibson & Sons Ltd.

Even companies who had their own spoutless shapes were licenced to produce the CUBE, for example, Gibson's WEMBLEY was joined by the CUBE in 1925. It was offered with all sorts of decoration; one interesting treatment was produced by overlaying a richly-coloured rose over a fawn or biscuit-coloured ground. Gibson's claimed to be not only the

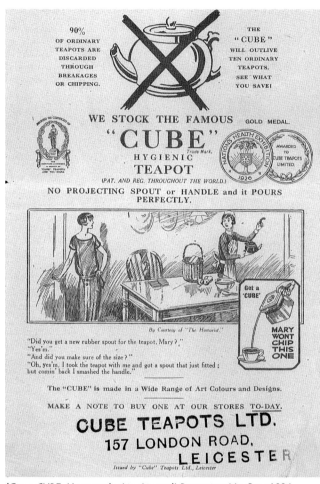

90%
OF ORDINARY
TEAPOTS ARE
DISCARDED
THROUGH
BREAKAGES
OR CHIPPING.

THE
"CUBE"
WILL OUTLIVE
TEN ORDINARY
TEAPOTS.
SEE WHAT
YOU SAVE!

WE STOCK THE FAMOUS   GOLD MEDAL.

"CUBE"
Trade Mark.
HYGIENIC
TEAPOT
(PAT. AND REG. THROUGHOUT THE WORLD.)

AWARDED
TO
CUBE TEAPOTS
LIMITED.

NO PROJECTING SPOUT or HANDLE and it POURS
PERFECTLY.

By Courtesy of "The Humorist."

"Did you get a new rubber spout for the teapot, Mary?"
"Yes'm."
"And did you make sure of the size?"
"Oh, yes'm, I took the teapot with me and got a spout that just fitted;
but comin' back I smashed the handle."

Get a
'CUBE'

MARY
WONT
CHIP
THIS
ONE

The "CUBE" is made in a Wide Range of Art Colours and Designs.

MAKE A NOTE TO BUY ONE AT OUR STORES TO-DAY.

CUBE TEAPOTS LTD.
157 LONDON ROAD,
LEICESTER

Issued by "Cube" Teapots Ltd., Leicester

'Get a CUBE. Mary won't chip this one'! Promotional leaflet, c1926.

Above, the alleged headquarters of the CUBE Teapots Company, Leicester.

Right, the reality was more modest!

largest makers of teapots in the world but also the producers of the widest variety of teapots in the trade. Their ingenuity knew no bounds and they continued to bring out new forms. The CAP-ALL, yet another patented safety teapot, with accessories, was introduced in 1929. As the name suggests, this model had a lock-lid, reminiscent of Lingard's HOOK-LID. Like the promoters of the CUBE, Gibson provided its retailers with a comprehensive range of advertising materials. A window display of a boy and girl supporting a teapot could be easily changed, as the teapot was real.

'A REAL SQUARE DEAL'

Apparently, the man behind the CUBE's American-style sales campaign was Percy Aspinall — one of the directors of the CUBE Teapots Co., Ltd. — who appears to have been largely responsible for the day-to-day running of the company. Aspinall was a true entrepreneur, demonstrated by his drive to establish a high profile for the CUBE teapot through an extensive press advertising campaign in *The Pottery Gazette* in 1926 and 1927. In addition to extolling the advantages of the CUBE over conventional teapots, the advertisements also emphasised the necessity of purchasing the genuine article, rather than an imitation of the CUBE:

> Evolution! The CUBE Teapot. Does not drip. Does not chip.
> Mr Buyer, when ordering Teapots see that they are CUBES.
> All other Teapots have either a projecting spout or handle.
> The CUBE has by far the largest sale of any Patent Teapot for the Home or Cafe equipment.
> The CUBE takes up the least room. Risk of breakage — nil.
> Artistic advertising display material is always available.

Percy Aspinall who managed the CUBE Teapots Co., Ltd. during the 1920s and 1930s.

The advertisement in *The Pottery Gazette* for September 1927 also warned against imitations:

> They're all pouring out with CUBE Teapots!
> Are you reaping your share of trade from these popular products? Remember, CUBE Teapots have the largest sale of any patent teapot in the world. Thousands are already using — thousands more about to buy...
> The latest CUBE Teapot has a new absolutely non-drip spout, cool roomy handle, improved lock-lid and clean wipe-out...
> Avoid imitations, look for the Regd. name CUBE on the bottom. Any other Teapot has either a projecting spout or handle.

Later advertisements in 1928 reiterated that the CUBE enjoyed the largest sale of any patent teapot in the world and was the only teapot without a projecting spout or handle.

By 1926 the CUBE had been modified with, as the advertisements claimed, an absolutely non-drip spout, the addition of a strainer and more generously recessed handle. These improvements to the design were necessary to keep the CUBE in the forefront and to stave off its rivals and their counter-claims. Seven points had obtained for the CUBE the largest sales of any patented teapot in the world.

1 **The Concealed Spout** cannot be broken off in a moment of careless handling and always pours perfectly.

2 **The Strainer** at the bottom of the spout, in the interior of the teapot, effectively keeps back the tea-leaves.

3 **The Wide Aperture** makes the CUBE the easiest teapot in the world to keep clean.

4 **The Sunken Lid** is another 'safety feature' of the CUBE. It cannot fall off while pouring.

5 **The Dainty Design** of the CUBE forms an artistic addition to the tea-table.

6 **The Built-In Handle** is never in danger of breakage, as it never gets in the way.

7 **The Square Shape** means greater convenience on both tea-tray and table. The CUBE occupies no more than its own standing room.

The new CUBE was featured in *The Pottery Gazette* in August 1926:

> The latest modification of the patent is seen in what is described as the 1926 CUBE teapot, which is provided with a somewhat more roomy handle than its predecessor, an improved lock-lid, an unrestricted opening and rounded

Mr. Buyer,
When ordering Teapots see that they are "CUBES." All other Teapots have either a projecting spout or handle.
THE "CUBE" has by far the largest sale of any Patent Teapot for the Home or Cafe equipment.
THE "CUBE" takes up the least room. Risk of breakage—nil.
Artistic advertising display material is always available.

WHY
CONTINUE TO ADVERTISE
"CUBE"
PERFECT POURING
TEAPOTS
when they already enjoy the largest sale of any patent teapot in the world?

It is to keep this fact before you

and to remind you that "Cube" Jugs and other equally popular articles of "Cube" Compact Teaware, Early Morning Sets, "Cube" Picnic Sets, etc., are made under licence by the following firms in their latest decorations:

E. BRAIN & CO., LTD.,
Foley China Works, Fenton, Staffs.
GEO. CLEWS & CO., LTD.,
Brownhills Pottery, Tunstall.
GIBSON & SONS, LTD.,
Albany & Harvey Potteries, Burslem.
T. G. GREEN & CO., LTD.,
Church Gresley Potteries, Burton-on-Trent.

GRIMWADES LTD.,
Winton Potteries, Stoke-on-Trent.
JACKSON & GOSLING,
Grosvenor Works, Longton, Staffs.
A. B. JONES & SONS,
Grafton Works, Longton, Staffs.
WEDGWOOD & CO., LTD.,
Tunstall, Stoke-on-Trent.

ALSO

CUBE TEAPOTS LTD., LEICESTER.

Telephone : 59724. Telegrams : "Cubes," Leicester.

ALL OTHER TEAPOTS HAVE PROJECTING SPOUTS OR HANDLES.

Patented and Registered throughout the World.

Top left, advertisement used in The Pottery Gazette *from c1926-1930.*

Left, advertisement from The Pottery Gazette, *September 1928.*

Above, advertisement from The Pottery Gazette, *January 1928.*

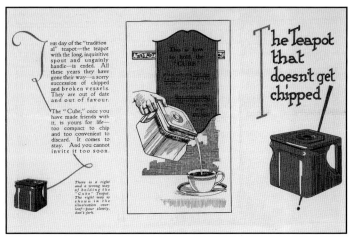

Top and above, promotional leaflets supplied by the CUBE Teapots Co., c1925-26.

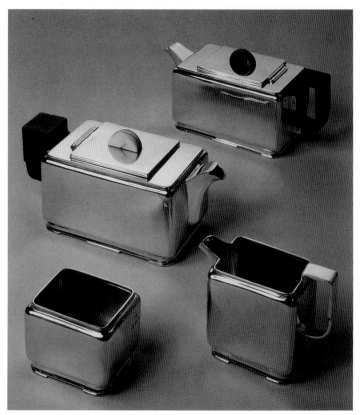

Cubic forms were not uncommon by the 1930s. This famous teaset was designed by Harold Stabler.

interior, facilitating an easy cleanout, and above all, a spout that is claimed to be absolutely non-drippable. The base of the spout is fitted with a tea-leaf strainer, which can be cleared instantaneously, and the large square opening beneath the lid admits easy access to the interior.

This article also reports that CUBE hot-water jugs and other

CUBE articles were already available. By 1926 the company's advertisements were featuring the new lines introduced by the CUBE Teapots Co: the CUBE Jugs, CUBE Compact Teaware, Early Morning Sets and CUBE Picnic Sets. By this stage the ingenious CUBE Egg Stand had arrived, which also doubled up as a rest for a cigar and ashtray! The company attempted to stay ahead of the competition with new products. There were plans to introduce a meat-dish, the 'Mount Carving Dish' (reg No.716458), which had a raised central area to allow the juices to collect in a large well at one end. Another ingenious device was the BETA bulb pot with holes for inserting labels.

The CUBE was also produced in metal, in electroplate on nickel silver and hammered pewter, by T. Willkinson and Sons

Above, CUBE Teapots Ltd., promotional leaflet, c1925-6, which relates to the price list (see p36).

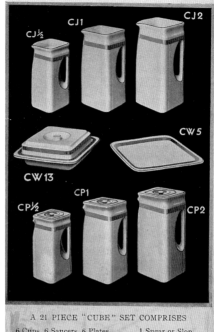

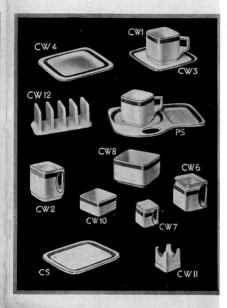

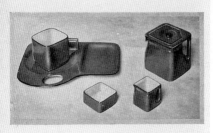

Promotional blotter for the CUBE Egg Stand, c1926.

A promotional leaflet showing the full range of CUBE Compact Teaware, c1925-6.

PRICE AND DESCRIPTION OF VARIOUS DECORATIONS	"Cube" Teapots 2½pt (24)	1½pt (30)	1pt (36)	¾pt (42)	½pt (48)	"Cube" Coffee Pots 2pt (24)	1½pt (30)	1pt (36)	½pt (42)	"Cube" Jugs 2pt (24)	1½pt (30)	1pt (36)	½pt (40)	"Cube" Teapot Stands L	M	S	"Cube" Sugars or Slops 2"	2½"	4"	"Cube" Creams 1oz	2oz	5oz	"Cube" Tea Cups & Saucers Encl. H'dle or O'side H'dle	'Cube' Plates 5 in.	'Cube' B & B's	'Cube' Toast Racks	'Cube' Palette & Cups	'Cube' Butter Con't'ners	'Cube' C'v'r'd M'f'ns
B0 Decorated Rock; Red Body ... per doz.	48/-	40/6	36/-	34/-	31/6				31/6	30/6	27/-	24/-						8/3			9/6								
B1 Plain Brown ... ,, ... ,,	34/-	28/6	26/6	24/-	21/-				21/-	21/6	19/6	16/-						6/3			7/6								
B2 Shaded Brown ... ,, ... ,,	36/-	31/-	28/6	26/-	22/6				22/6	23/-	21/-	17/-						9/6			11/-								
B50 Plain Green ... ,, ... ,,																													
B100 Plain White ... ,, ... ,,	42/-	33/-	28/6	25/-	21/-	31/6	27/-	18/6	13/6	24/-	20/-	13/-	10/-	12/-	10/-	7/-	3/-	5/-	8/6	3/-	5/-	7/-	14/6	7/-	14/-	11/6	24/-	13/-	31/6
B300-4 Salmon, Blue, Green and Buff Dipped	48/-	40/6	36/-	32/-	28/-	40/-	33/-	24/-	20/-	30/-	24/-	18/-	13/6				4/-	7/-	11/6	5/-	7/-	10/6					15/-	16/3	
Ditto with Gold Lines	60/-	51/-	42/-	38/-	33/-	48/-	39/-	30/-	23/-	37/6	30/-	23/-	18/-				5/-	7/-	14/-	6/-	8/-	11/-					17/6	20/-	
B330 White and Lines, Gold, Blue, Green	48/-	40/6	36/-	32/-	28/-	39/-	31/6	23/-	16/6	30/-	24/-	18/-	13/6	19/-	15/-	12/-	4/-	7/-	10/6	5/-	7/-	9/6	24/-	15/-	19/-	15/-	27/-	15/-	39/-
B310 Tangerine B312 Apple Green / B313 Yellow B314 Turkish Blue / B343 B344 Fancy Borders / B426/7 Hand Craft Painted / B434 etc. Coloured Apples, Plums, etc. / B328 Check Border / B348 Hunting Scenes, Black Finish / B326 Mazarine Blue Band and Gilt / B414 Indian Tree	54/-	48/-	40/6	36/-	31/6	42/6	35/-	27/-	19/-	32/6	28/-	20/-	15/-	20/-	16/-	12/-	5/-	7/-	12/6	5/6	8/-	11/-	28/-	16/-	20/-	15/-	36/-	17/-	45/-
B415/416/418/421/327/357, Litho Coloured Base (See separate sheet)	63/-	54/-	48/-	42/-	39/-	52/6	45/-	36/-	27/-	45/-	36/-	27/-	20/-	24/-	19/-	15/-	5/6	7/6	15/-	6/6	8/6	12/-	39/-	23/-	27/-	20/-	45/-	21/-	57/-
B423/424/425 Dipped Decorated	66/-	57/-	51/-	47/-	40/6																								

LATEST "CUBE" NOVELTY: UTILITY EGG CUP ON STAND. SPECIAL DECORATIONS 9/- PER DOZEN.

Price list, c1925, issued by CUBE Teapots Limited, Leicester.

CUBE TEAPOTS

Telephone: CENTRAL 59726

LIMITED

Telegrams: "CUBES" Leicester

GOLD MEDAL — AWARDED TO CUBE TEAPOTS LIMITED — NATIONAL HEALTH EXHIBITION 1926

LEICESTER

SPECIAL REVISED NETT TRADE PRICE LIST

	"Cube" Teapots 2½pt (24)	1½pt (30)	1pt (36)	¾pt (42)	½pt (48)	'Cube' Coffee Pots 2pt (24)	1½pt (30)	1pt (36)	½pt (42)	'Cube' Jugs 2pt (24)	1½pt (30)	1pt (36)	½pt (42)	Cube Teapot Stands L	M	S	'Cube' Sugars 1oz	2oz	5oz	'Cube' Creams 1oz	2oz	5oz	'Cube' Tea Cups & Saucers Encl. H'dle	O'side H'dle	'Cube' Plates 3 in.	4 in.	Slop B'sins	B & B's	Egg Cups	Toast Racks	Palette & Cups	Butter Con't'ners	C'v'r'd M'f'ns
B0 Decorated Rock ... per doz.	32/-	27/-	24/-	22/6	21/-				21/-				12/9	15/-	15/-	12/6	9/6			6/6					7/6								
B1 Plain Brown ... ,,	22/6	19/-	17/6	16/-	14/-				12/9					9/6	9/-	7/-	5/-			6/-													
B2 Shaded Brown ... ,,	24/-	20/6	18/9	17/3	15/-				15/-					11/-	11/-	9/-	7/-			7/6					8/6								
B50 Plain Green ... ,,																																	
B100 Plain White ... ,,	28/-	21/9	19/-	16/6	13/6	25/-	21/-	14/6	10/6	19/-	16/-	10/-	7/6	9/6	7/6	5/3	2/-	3/3	5/-	3/6	5/6		11/3	11/3	5/6	6/6	11/-		3/-	9/-	18/-	10/-	25/-
B300-4 Salmon, Blue, Green and Buff Dipped ... ,,	32/-	27/-	24/-	21/-	18/6	32/-	26/-	19/-	13/6	24/-	19/-	14/-	10/6				3/-	5/-	7/-	3/6	5/-	7/6			9/-							13/-	
Ditto with Gold Lines ... ,,	39/-	33/-	28/-	25/-	22/-	38/-	31/-	24/-	18/-	31/-	24/-	18/-	14/-				4/-	5/6	8/-	4/6	6/-	8/6			11/-					5/6	14/-	15/6	
B330 White & Lines, Gold, Blue, Green ... ,,	32/-	27/-	24/-	21/-	18/6		25/-	18/-	13/-	24/-	19/-	14/-	10/6	15/-	12/-	9/-	3/-	5/-	7/-	3/6	5/-	7/6	19/-	18/6	11/6	15/-	3/6	11/-	21/-		11/6	30/-	
B310 Tangerine B312 Apple Green / B313 Yellow B314 Turkish Blue / B343 B344 B346 Fancy Borders / B426/7 Hand Craft Painted / B434 etc. Coloured Apples, Plums, etc.	34/-	29/-	25/-	22/6	19/6	34/-	28/-	21/-	15/-	26/-	22/-	16/-	12/-	16/-	12/6	9/6	4/-	5/6	8/-	4/3	6/-	8/6	20/6	20/-	13/-	9/6	16/6	5/6	11/6	29/-	13/6	38/6	
B328 Check Border ... ,,	33/-	28/-	25/-	22/6	19/6	33/-	27/-	20/-	14/-	25/-	21/-	15/-	11/-	15/-	12/-	9/-	3/6	5/6	7/6	4/-	5/6	8/-	19/6	19/-	12/-	9/-	15/9	5/-	11/6	27/6	12/6	35/-	
B348 Hunting Scenes, Black Finish / B326 Mazarine Blue Band and Gilt / B414 Indian Tree	36/-	32/-	27/-	24/-	21/-	34/-	28/-	21/-	15/-	26/-	22/-	16/-	12/-	16/-	12/6	9/6	4/-	5/6	8/-	4/3	6/-	8/6	20/6	20/-	13/-	9/6	15/9	5/6	11/6	29/-	12/6	35/-	
B415/416/418/421/327/357, Litho Coloured Base (See separate sheet)	42/-	36/-	31/-	28/-	25/-	42/-	35/-	26/-	20/-	36/-	28/-	21/-	16/-	19/-	15/-	12/-	4/3	5/9	8/6	5/-	6/6	9/6	30/6	30/-	17/6	12/-	21/-	7/-	16/-	38/-	16/6	45/-	
B423/424/425 Dipped Decorated ... ,,	44/-	38/-	33/-	31/-	27/-	43/-	36/-	29/-	24/-	38/-	32/-	26/-	22/-				5/-	6/6	9/-	5/6	7/-	9/6											

Prices for other Decorations or Badging upon application.
ALL GOODS CARRIAGE FORWARD EX WORKS.

PATENTED AND REGISTERED THROUGHOUT THE WORLD

Revised price list, c1930, issued by CUBE Teapots Limited, Leicester. Note the reduced prices, perhaps resulting from the Depression of the late 1920s.

CUBE Teapots and Teaware leaflet issued by CUBE Teapots Ltd., manufactured by T.G. Green, c1925-26.

"CUBE" TEAPOTS

REGD. TRADE MARK

Floral Border and Lines.
B346
SIZES 24 30 36 42 48
7/3 6/3 5/3 4/6 4/-

Plain White.
B100
SIZES 24 30 36 42 48
4/3 3/9 3/5 3/2 2/11

Dipped Art Shades.
SIZES 24 30 36 42 48
B300 Cornflower Blue ⎫
B301 Salmon Pink ... ⎬ 6/3 5/3 4/6 4/- 3/9
B302 Buff ... ⎪
B304 Pea Green ... ⎭
As above with gold lines 7/6 6/6 5/6 4/9 4/3

White and Lines.
SIZES 24 30 36 42 48
B330 White with gold lines ⎫
B331 ,, ,, blue ,, ⎬ 6/3 5/3 4/6 4/- 3/9
B332 ,, ,, green ,, ⎭
B330

Silhouette Design.
B348
Hunting Design, Black on White.
SIZES 24 30 36 42 48
7/6 6/6 5/6 4/9 4/3

Fruit Border and Lines.
B343
SIZES 24 30 36 42 48
7/3 6/3 5/3 4/6 4/-

Plain Brown.
B1
SIZES 24 30 36 42 48
3/6 2/11 2/6 2/3 1/11

Shaded Brown.
B2
SIZES 24 30 36 42 48
4/- 3/6 3/2 2/9 2/6

Plain Green.
B50
SIZES 24 30 36 42 48
4/- 3/6 3/2 2/9 2/6

Mazarine Blue Band, Gold Line.
B326
SIZES 24 30 36 42 48
7/6 6/6 5/6 4/9 4/3

Black Check Border.
B328
SIZES 24 30 36 42 48
7/3 6/3 5/3 4/6 4/-

Floral Border and Lines.
B344
SIZES 24 30 36 42 48
7/3 6/3 5/3 4/6 4/-

Solid Art Colours.
SIZES 24 30 36 42 48
B310 Tangerine ... ⎫
B311 Kingfisher Blue ... ⎪
B312 Apple Green ... ⎬ 7/3 6/3 5/3 4/6 4/-
B313 Yellow ... ⎪
B314 Powder Blue ... ⎪
B315 Mauve ... ⎭

Lustres.
SIZES 24 30 36 42 48
B320 Pale Blue Lustre ⎫
B321 Green Lustre ... ⎬ 7/6 6/6 5/6 4/9 4/3
B322 Orange Lustre ... ⎭

"CUBE" TEAPOT LIDS
At a third the price of Teapots

PLEASE NOTE CAPACITY and DIMENSIONS					
SIZES	24	30	36	42	48
Capacity in Pints ...	2½	1½	1	¾	½
Cubic measurement, inches	5½	4½	4	3½	3

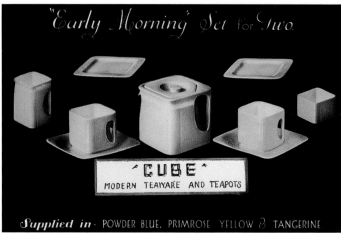

"Early Morning" Set for Two.

'CUBE' MODERN TEAWARE AND TEAPOTS

Supplied in - POWDER BLUE, PRIMROSE YELLOW & TANGERINE

QUEEN MARY

CUNARD WHITE STAR

Top, CUBE Teapots Ltd., illustrations to the revised price list of the later 1920s.

Above, promotional postcard from the late 1920s. CUBE Teaware was available in six 'Art Colours': powder blue, primrose yellow, tangerine, kingfisher blue, apple green and mauve.

Right, a rare colour image of the Queen Mary with a table set with CUBES in the foreground. The cabin-class long gallery in its original form, 1936.

Ivory banded CUBES for the Queen Mary *and* Queen Elizabeth. *First supplied by Jackson & Gosling; these examples by Brain's Foley China, supplied by Stonier's, 1950s.*

Above, Copeland's Currents. No CUBES have been found in this pattern used alongside Minton's Cuckoo and Plant's Bird of Paradise on Cunarders from the late 1920s.

Above right, Jackson & Gosling Grosvenor China, Rose pattern. This pattern was also made by Foley Bone China in the 1950s.

Right, Minton's Cuckoo pattern which can be easily confused with Plant's Bird of Paradise.

Ivory banded ware on an original Cunard tray (c1936), Foley Bone China, 1950s.

Matching ivory banded ware, John Maddock & Sons.

Clews stoneware, matt oatmeal CUBES for the Queen Mary, *marked Cunard White Star, c1936.*

Clews stoneware, glossy brown souvenir pieces for the Queen Mary, *marked Cunard White Star, supplied by Stonier's, c1936.*

A range of Cunard pieces with gold banding. Those by Myott, and Fielding's Crown Devon were for the QE2, c1969. Sadler's provided plain CUBES in the 1950s and 1960s. The jug with the Rose Bud pattern has not been linked to a specific ship.

Plant's lace-like VIP Tuscan Bone China for the first-class passengers on the Queen Elizabeth, 1950s.

Commonwealth & Dominion, later Port Line, Cornflower pattern, Gibson and Hammersley.

Teaset by Sadler's, with defaced Cunard backstamps, possibly not for a Cunarder, 1950s.

Sadler's, possibly a Cunard pattern.

Bibby Line jug by Grimwades.

Unmarked plain white bone china and earthenware CUBES. The most commonly found CUBE today (many of these were seconds). The full range was available by 1925.

CUBES by Clews: second from left, silvered teapot, third from left, lustred teapot, 1930s.

CUBE teacup, saucer and plate by Brain's Foley Bone China, late 1920s.

Brain's Foley Bone China teaset, late 1920s.

Brain's Foley Bone China teaset, late 1920s.

Brain's Foley Bone China, shagreen effect, late 1920s.

Grimwades' earthenware: far left, Ming pattern with the Dragon mark.

Above left, CUBE for the coronation of Queen Elizabeth II, 1953.

Above right, earthenware CUBES by Gibson & Sons.

Left, T.G. Green earthenware. These teapots did not always carry the company backstamp with the CUBE trademark.

Two handpainted patterns by Jackson & Gosling, bone china, late 1920s/1930s.

Monochrome earthenwares: from left, CUBE by Arthur Wood, pre-1925; three CUBES, with CUBE Teapots Ltd. Leicester, backstamp, 1930s/1950s.

CUBES by Wedgwood & Co., 1930s. CUBE with violets pattern also carries Hammersley backstamp.

CUBE Teapots Ltd. Leicester, backstamp only.

Plant's Tuscan Bone China teaset with the Bird of Paradise pattern, used on the Cunarders from the late 1920s.

Late CUBES with projecting knops: left, Royal Crownford, Staffs; right, Burleigh Ironstone.

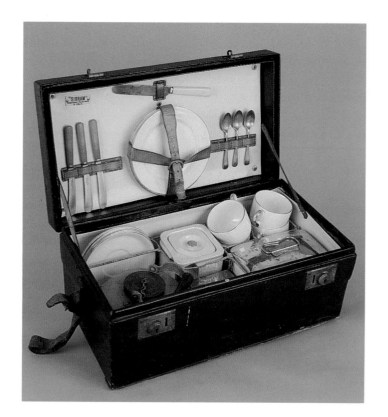

S.Y.P. by Wedgwood.

DUB-L-DEKR (DUBL-DEKR) by Clews.

Top and above, CUBE picnic set, note the conventional shape of the cup and saucer.

The COSY teapot or UnIversal Jug, made from 1922. Left, Wood & Sons, Burslem, right, Elkington plate.

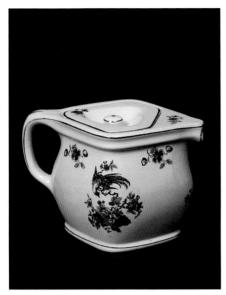

Rubian Art Ware teapot, Regd. No.730,719, made from 1927.

The HANDY HEXAGON by James Sadler & Son, from 1921.

G.M.C. manufactured by C.M. Creyke & Sons, from 1923.

The HANDY HEXAGON by James Sadler & Son, from 1921.

Silver-plated teapot with ebony handle by T. Wilkinson & Sons, from c1925.

Cane-handled teapot by T. Wilkinson & Sons, the sugar bowl, Elkington plate from c1925.

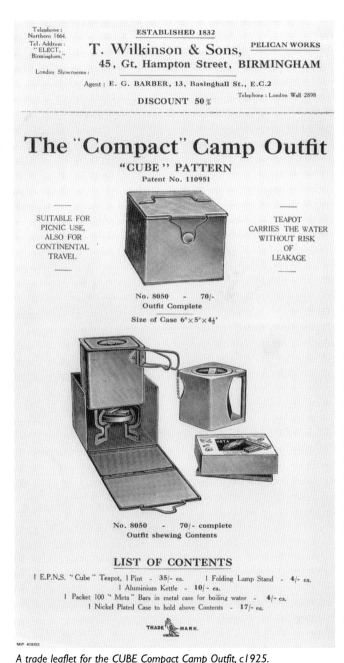

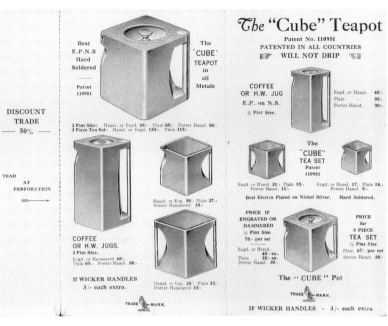

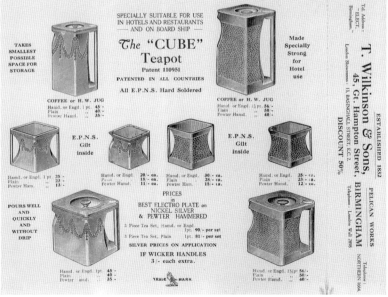

A trade leaflet for the CUBE Compact Camp Outfit, c1925.

The CUBE range in EPNS, available from c1925. Although this trade pamphlet mentions shipping lines there is no evidence to suggest metal CUBES were used on the Cunarders.

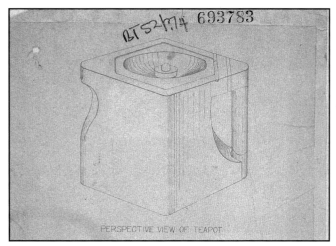

Regd. Shape 693783, 1922, CUBE teapot for production in metal.

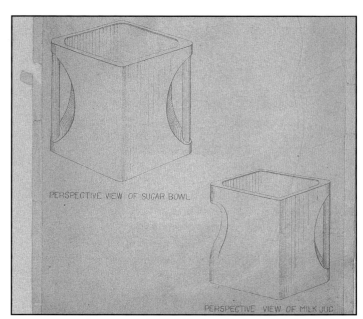

Regd. Shape 693783, 1922, CUBE sugar bowl and milk or cream jug for production in metal.

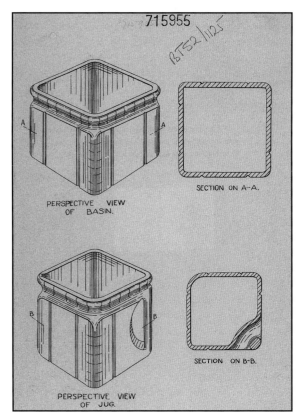

Regd. Shape 715955, 1925 for CUBE bowl and jug. This number is seen on many CUBE pieces.

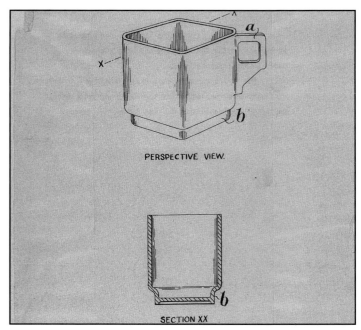

Regd. Shape 717709, 1925 for a CUBE cup. This is quite different to the cup that went into production. (All images supplied by the Public Records Office)

of Birmingham. Their Pelican Works produced a wide range of CUBE products including teasets, with plain, hammered or engraved surfaces. They even produced the Compact Camp Outfit (Patent No.110951), suitable for picnics and continental travel. Such was the success of the CUBE Teapots Company that by c1927 they had a London office at 35 Oxford Street. The London office appears to have been given up during the harsh trading conditions of the Depression years. Advertisements also indicate that by the end of the 1930s the Leicester Showrooms had moved from 157 London Road to 29 Newarke Street.

There is no doubt that the CUBE shapes were seen to be bright and new. The company was keen to emphasise this in its advertisements, appealing to a young and progressive-minded clientele:

> The furniture of 1930 reflects the very best creative tendencies of this age, being severely simple in line and form and employing geometric ornament with wise restraint. This distinctive CUBE ware is destined to a definite place in the traditions of English pottery, harmonising with modern decoration, at the same time aiming at economy in space.

Health and hygiene were also emphasised in the CUBE's marketing strategy. The CUBE was awarded the Certificate of the Institute of Hygiene, and in 1926 the firm secured a Gold

The SERVICE teapot, 'Buyer's Notes', The Pottery Gazette, January 1927.

EVERCLEAN PATENT HYGENIC teapot, James Sadler & Sons, from The Pottery Gazette, February 1936.

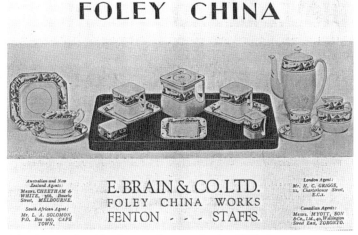

Advertisement from The Pottery Gazette, October 1928, illustrating a morning set in CUBIST LANDSCAPE. Note the alternative 'normal' shapes.

Advertisement from The Pottery Gazette, June 1927, for Wade's COMPACTO.

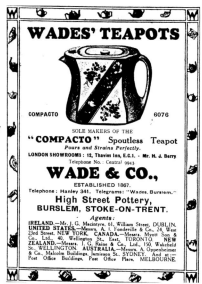

Undated advertisement from c1930.

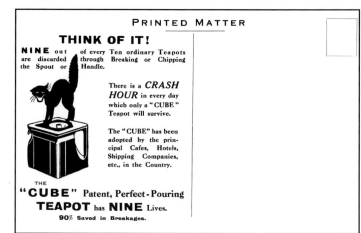

Reverse of promotional postcard mentioning the use of CUBES by shipping companies, c1930.

Advertisement from The Pottery Gazette, January 1931. Note the inclusion of Cunard.

Advertisement from The Pottery Gazette, September 1932.

Advertisement from The Pottery Gazette, September 1933.

Medal at the Nation's Health Exhibition. Advertisements from 1926 bear the legend HYGIENIC CUBE TEAWARE. The company also had a stand at the Nation's Food Exhibition.

Foley China adopted CUBE forms in order to appeal to this emerging market for progressive tastes, emphasising in their marketing both utility and beauty, for example in *The Pottery Gazette* in 1928:

> it is at once apparent that the manufacturers of this particular brand of bone china are leaving no stone unturned to bring out designs which are not only thoroughly appreciative of the trend of modern furnishings but also in strict conformity with the simplicity of style and dignified plainness of shape which were accepted many years ago at the Foley china works as the principle worthy of being adhered to.

Evidently this pottery only produced shapes and patterns which were simple and of good taste, 'eschewing everything that is unnecessary in the direction of elaboration'. Foley was a name associated with utility and the firm did not seek to manufacture anything that was of ornamental value only. Foley had endeavoured to give the public a lead, by pruning their range of shapes and patterns in table china, and demonstrating how dignity and good taste could be retained though much might be saved in household labour and unnecessary expense. Their shapes were easy to clean and the designs neat; if the buyer wanted something more ornate or gaudy he should seek it elsewhere. The manufacturers of Foley, E. Brain and Co., had responded to the new trends for bright colours and geometric forms by introducing a CUBE range with bold patterns, CUBIST LANDSCAPE and CUBIST SUNFLOWERS. *The Pottery Gazette* noted that these were both smart and original:

> these are patterns in which the employment of the brightest possible colours is allied to an altogether new style of decorative manipulation. Such designs are true to the instincts of the age for which they seek to cater – a little advanced it may be, but someone is bound to give the public a lead.

While somewhat daring, even courageous, *The Pottery Gazette* recognised that Foley was attempting to bring ceramic design up-to-date. It was hoped that the public would not fail to appreciate their efforts! However, it would be fair to say that such boldness was more acceptable in pottery than in

bone china, as the former was cheaper and, consequently, manufacturers could afford to respond to high fashion and still cater for a mass market. Bone china was expected to have a longer life so, hence, more traditional forms were wanted. Recognising this, Foley also produced the CUBE with traditional patterns, which although pretty often compromised the severity of the shape.

By 1928 the list of firms producing the CUBE under licence had also increased and now included:

> E. Brain & Co., Ltd., Foley China
> George Clews & Co., Ltd., Brownhills Pottery
> Gibson & Sons, Ltd., Albany and Harvey Works
> T.G. Green & Co., Ltd., Church Gresley Potteries
> Grimwades Ltd., Winton Potteries
> Jackson & Gosling, Grosvenor Works
> A.B. Jones & Sons, Grafton Works
> Wedgwood & Co., Ltd.

A brief history of each of the factories that produced the CUBE under licence is listed on pages 77-81 together with details of patterns.

Even the forming of the CUBE Teapots Company did not deter rivals. In 1927, Wade, Heath & Co., launched its COMPACTO spoutless teapot. The COMPACTO combined the, by then typical, spoutless profile with a sunken-lid and recessed handle and was designed to meet the needs of the catering trade. Wade, Heath & Co., better known as Wade's, also marketed a teapot known as the KEW, which was less radical in design but still had a cubic look.

Bursley Ltd., Crown Pottery, one of the associated concerns of Wood and Sons, although not a studio pottery as such was, according to *The Pottery Gazette* in January 1927, 'as near to it as any really practical and commercial concern is ever likely to get'. A studio atmosphere prevailed, individualism was encouraged and handwork loomed large in the firm's everyday output. The art director was Frederick Arthur Rhead (1857-1933) one of the most famous figures in the potteries, and the father of Charlotte Rhead. He had already produced artistic wares at Wardle and designed a range of handpainted wares for Wileman's Foley Art Pottery. At the turn of the century he had encouraged tube-lining in the potteries, of which his daughter was a famous exponent. At the Crown Pottery, ornamental wares were the backbone of the trade.

90% saved in Breakages

A REAL "SQUARE DEAL"

"**CUBE**" Teapots have concealed spouts, built-in handles and sunken lids. Consequently the "**CUBE**" Teapot has a long life and is not exposed to chipping and breaking at the vital parts.

Also the square and solid design of the "**CUBE**" Teapot makes it easy to clean, safe in storage and free from dripping or leakage while in use.

Already adopted by leading hotels, cafés and restaurants in all parts. Also standard equipment on "Cunard" and and other liners.

Send for free details and quotations:

CUBE TEAPOTS LTD.
29 Newarke St., Leicester

Advertisement from the 1930s, picking up on Franklin D. Roosevelt's slogan, the 'New Deal'. Note the new address.

Remember the CUBE Patent Teapot with Non-Drip Spout and Lock Lid is obtainable only from:
CUBE TEAPOTS LTD., LEICESTER, ENGLAND
and the well-known firms making under licence.
Anyone selling or passing off any other teapot as a CUBE is thereby rendered liable to legal proceedings. So avoid all imitations and look for the genuine CUBE backstamp.

The CUBE also made good use of the honours it was accorded – the Certificate of the Institute of Hygiene and the Gold Medal at the Nation's Health Exhibition – and both were incorporated in the advertisements. By the early 1930s the CUBE was the obvious choice for commercial use and could be found in Lyons Corner Houses and on the Rhodesian Railways. Advertisements superimposed the CUBE over a conventional teapot, emphasising its modern shape, 'severely simple in line and form, harmonising with modern decoration'. Evidently the CUBE had nine lives, for nine out of every ten ordinary teapots were discarded through 'breaking or chipping the spout or handle'. The CUBE was a 'A REAL SQUARE DEAL'.

THE CUNARD LINE

The CUBE made its first appearance at sea in the later 1920s. Advertisements with the legend 'used as standard equipment by Cunard and other lines, leading cafés and hotels' started appearing in *The Pottery Gazette* from August 1930. Promotional pamphlets from c1925-26 feature the CUBE as

Although set up to produce artistic items, this company felt the need to produce a spoutless teapot, the SERVICE. Made in three sizes, fitted with a double strainer and interchangeable lock cover, the design was an admirable shape for stacking.

The success of their HANDY HEXAGON encouraged Sadler's to introduce yet another improved teapot, the EVERCLEAN Patent Hygenic Teapot, in 1936. This new teapot for the catering trade had a special spout with a wide opening for easy cleaning. As usual it also claimed to be non-drip.

An advertisement in *The Pottery Gazette* of September 1932, indicates that the CUBE Teapots Company still considered any imitations to be a threat to their trade:

Minton's Cuckoo pattern was supplied to the Cunarders before 1934. It was also used in the Lyons Corner Houses.

Tea on the Mauretania using Plant's Tuscan China, Bird of Paradise pattern. This old photograph was actually used in promotional material for the second Mauretania (1939). The new ship used the CUBE shape but with the simple banded pattern first supplied to the Queen Mary (1936). (Southampton Cultural Services)

the 'ideal teapot' for every condition everywhere – hotel, café, shipboard and the home. Minton's supplied their *Cuckoo* pattern in bone china to the great Cunarders, *Aquitania* and *Mauretania*. CUBE shapes were not adopted in this design until c1926/1928. Sales were not conducted directly with the manufacturers but through specialist suppliers, like Reynold's and Stonier's of Liverpool. R.H. & S.L. Plant's Tuscan China *Bird of Paradise*, a pattern very similar to *Cuckoo* but including a bird in flight, was also used, notably for Souvenir ware. The pieces seen bore the pattern numbers 9030 and 9033. Contemporary photographs clearly show both patterns in use. Copeland's also supplied a similar pattern, *Currents* (R4535). This was introduced by the firm in 1912 and was in use on Cunard ships by 1914. In addition to the fully-coloured pattern, a black and white version was also available. All these patterns, which look so alike, were in use before 1934 and carry the original Cunard mark. Copeland's also supplied the White Star Line and Canadian Pacific Steamships, or CPS. Jackson & Gosling, an associate of Copeland, began supplying Cunard in the early 1930s.

The CUBE was not exclusively used on transatlantic ships. The Commonwealth and Dominion Line, which operated from 1914 until 1937 when it became the Port Line (1937-1981) used CUBE shapes supplied by Gibson's decorated with the *Cornflower* pattern (PN6034) and marked Hammersley (England), which dates them to the period 1912-1939. After 1939, 'Made in England' was added. The *Cornflower* pattern was also used on non-CUBE shapes and both are illustrated. The Commonwealth and Dominion Line serviced the Australian routes. In 1916 it was taken over by Cunard but run separately, as the Cunard Line Australasian Service, Commonwealth and Dominion Line. The fleet consisted of cargo ships which carried only twelve passengers. If a ship carried more than this number a doctor was required. The china was used by the ship's company, as well as the paying passengers and, despite the small number of passengers, souvenir pieces were produced. All the ships in the line were called after a port, for example, *Port Caroline, Port Auckland*. By 1970 the line was used mainly for cargo (Cunard Cargo Shipping) and it ceased operations in 1981.

The Bibby Line primarily ran passenger and troop services to the colonies – Burma was a typical destination. The line,

Tourist-class lounge on the Aquitania. Plant's Tuscan China, *Bird of Paradise pattern in use, c1930. (Liverpool University)*

Modern styling aboard the Queen Mary. *A private dining room laid out with CUBES. Vanessa Bell's picture is on the right. (Queen Mary Foundation)*

RMS Queen Mary *berthed alongside the* Aquitania. *This photograph illustrates the relative size of the transatlantic liners.*

one of the oldest, operated from 1807 to 1990. The name Bibby is still seen, but the business is now concerned with container shipping and road haulage. A typical Bibby Line ship, the *Derbyshire 2*, launched in 1935, carried 291 first-class passengers. The *Devonshire* carried 401 first-class and 90 second-class passengers, and 1,150 troops in 1939. Many of the ships in the fleet began their lives as cargo vessels and were later converted. The *Dorset,* for example, launched in 1920 was converted in 1927. It carried 112 first-class, 58 second-class, 108 troop families in third-class, plus 1,450 troops. The CUBE shapes made for the Bibby Line carry the Line's crest with a

green leaf pattern. The jug illustrated was made by Grimwades and carries the standard post-1926 mark.

The CUBE's pre-eminent position was ensured by the contract for Cunard's great transatlantic liner, the *Queen Mary*. According to *The Ship Builder and Marine Engine Builder*, CUBE shapes were chosen for the *Queen Mary*, the pride of the Cunard fleet, 'because of the economies in stowage and the reduction in breakages which such shapes have proved by experience to possess.' It had already proved most effective on the *Aquitania* and *Mauretania*, as its flat sides made it perfect for racking and stacking at sea. By 1936, the CUBE

Above, the Aquitania (1914) used historical styling designed to appeal to an American clientele. The CUBE must have looked a little out of place. (Southampton Cultural Services)

Left, passengers relax with afternoon tea on the promenade deck of the Aquitania, c1930. Plant's Tuscan China, Bird of Paradise pattern. (Liverpool University)

A birthday aboard the Aquitania *or* Mauretania, *c1930. CUBE shapes can be clearly seen in Plant's Tuscan China,* Bird of Paradise *pattern.*

might have appeared a little dated, compared to the streamlined designs emanating from America. Indeed, by the following year, G.M. Creyke & Sons were offering a streamlined design known as the T-FLO. Although, as *The Pottery Gazette* wrote, 'streamlining speeds up sales in 1937', this design was obviously not as practical for life at sea.

Transatlantic travel had been developing since the mid-nineteenth century. The White Star Line or Oceanic Steam Navigation Company was founded in 1869 by Thomas Henry Ismay (1837-1899), with William Imrie. Ismay, who turned down a baronetcy, was known for his generosity and his collection of British paintings, which included works by Sir John Everett Millais, Sir David Wilkie and John Phillip. The White Star Line operated the *Homeric,* the *Olympic* and the ill-fated *Titanic.* The *Oceanic* entered the Liverpool to New York Service on 2nd March 1871 and was followed by the *Britannic*

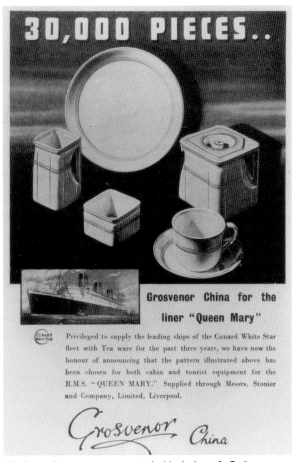

The bone china teaware was supplied by Jackson & Gosling, a subsidiary of Copeland & Son. Such advertisements appeared in The Ocean Times, *the newspaper produced by Cunard.*

and *Germanic* in 1874 and 1875. The *Oceanic 2*, built in 1899 in consultation with the architect Richard Norman Shaw, was then the largest and most luxurious ship in the world. In 1907 the company moved from Liverpool to Southampton. The next generation of liners was built for size and greater comfort rather than speed. The *Olympic* was launched in 1911 and was followed by the *Titanic*. After the First World War the fleet included the *Majestic,* originally the German *Bismark,* the largest passenger liner afloat in the 1920s, and the *Homeric*. In total there were fifteen ships, including the smaller *Doric, Pittsburgh* and *Laurentic.*

In 1934 the White Star Line joined forces with Cunard, a company with an equally impressive record. This merger was a government requirement in order to secure funds for constructing the new super liners, the *Queen Mary* and her sister ship, the *Queen Elizabeth*. Cunard had been established in 1840 and the *Britannia* was its first steamer. The *Umbria* and *Etruria* were launched in 1884 and broke all speed records. With the new century, Cunard launched a series of magnificent liners including the *Lusitania* in 1907, lost in the First World War, the *Mauretania*, which held the Blue Riband until 1929, and the *Aquitania*. This ship was launched in 1913, and immediately seconded for wartime duties. After the war the German-built *Berengaria* was added to the fleet which, along with the *Aquitania* and *Mauretania*, established the Cunard Express Service between Southampton, Cherbourg and New York in 1919. The *Berengaria* at 52,002 tons and the

Stoneware breakfast sets and morning sets by George Clews for both Queens *and the second* Mauretania.

Banded dinner ware from John Maddock & Sons, and gold-printed Tuscan Bone China from Plant's for the Queen Elizabeth.

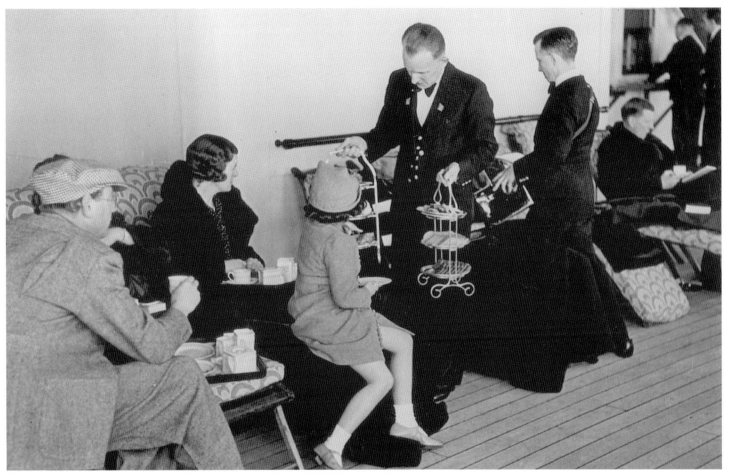

Tea time: passengers on the promenade deck of the Queen Mary, c1938. (Hulton Getty)

Aquitania at 45,647 tons were the giants of the fleet. During the 1920s, plans were drawn up to replace these liners with new, state-of-the-art ships but, just as construction began, the Great Depression hit. The first of the *Queens* was delayed by 27 months and was not launched until 1934 with her sister ship planned for operation by 1940. The *Queen Elizabeth* was launched in 1938 but by 1939 she was being prepared for war service. Finally fitted for commercial use, her maiden commercial voyage was in October 1946. At 83, 673 tons she was the world's largest liner. On December 31st 1949 Cunard took over the White Star Line, and only the *Britannic* and *Georgic* still sailed as White Star.

Encouraged by the vast amount of new tonnage built after the First World War, Atlantic tourism became an established habit through the introduction of tourist-class accommodation which offered many amenities previously associated with first class and, perhaps most important of all, reasonable passage rates which brought a holiday in North America or Europe within the reach of an enormous new public. It was in the 1920s that cruising came to the forefront and, as recreational facilities had to be improved, this certainly influenced ship design. Swimming pools and large areas of open deck for games were required – the *Aquitania* was the first to have a permanent swimming pool. The *Franconia*,

The Queen Mary *promenade deck, late 1940s. (Liverpool University)*

launched in 1923 and the *Carinthia*, in 1925, were primarily designed for cruising. A world cruise aboard the *Franconia* lasted nearly five months. Launched in 1949, the *Caronia* known as the 'Green Goddess' because of her green hull, kept the tradition of luxury cruising alive in the period of post-war austerity, carrying only first-class passengers. The *Queen Mary* represented a new and bold departure in terms of design and appointments:

> period style has been discarded in favour of a restrained modernism. The rooms will be perfectly satisfying to the most cosmopolitan conceptions of culture and good taste and at the same time convey the atmosphere of restfulness

and comfort associated with the most dignified British country homes.

The *Queen Mary* was the first British liner to adopt a modern style. The interiors of the *Aquitania*, fitted immediately after the First World War, resembled a period country house. There was a Palladian salon in the first-class accommodation and a Carolean smoking-room, the rich oak-beamed ceiling of the latter suggesting an old wooden battleship. The design of this room evoked the Restoration period, as it was adapted from the old Greenwich Hospital. The first-class restaurant assumed the style of Louise XVI:

The long gallery of the Parthia (1947/8) showing the Rose pattern still in use. (Liverpool University)

The Carmania (1954/1963), the renamed Saxonia; first-class lounge with CUBES still in use, late 1960s. (Liverpool University)

English country houses are the true home of old and distinguished families, truly 'country' houses, splendid monuments of the earlier periods of architecture and decoration softened and made lovely by reverent use. The *Aquitania* is like an English country house. Its great rooms are perfect replicas of the fine salons and handsome apartments that one finds in the best of old English manor halls. The decorations are too restrained ever to be oppressive in their magnificence. There is no effort to create an atmosphere of feverish gaiety by means of ornate and colourful furnishing. The ship breathes an air of elegance that is very gratifying to the type of people who are her passengers.

This description was evidently intended to appeal to the American passenger. Even the *Franconia*, launched in 1923, was still decorated in historical styles. By the mid-1930s a modern approach was necessitated by the success of the great French transatlantic liners, the *Paris* (1921), the *Ile de France* (1927) and the *Normandie* (1932). The French ships established the 'ocean liner style' with the *Ile de France* and the *Normandie* benefiting from the latest in Art Deco styling. By the 1930s the High Art Deco of the 1920s had been tempered by Modernism and the Depression. The *moderne* style was in many ways a compromise but it appealed to the

Breakfast in style in a first-class cabin on the Queen Elizabeth. *Note the thermos jug with CUBE jug and bowl. (Liverpool University)*

masses and was associated with the glamour of Hollywood. The *Queen Mary* was 'modern without being ultra modern'. The decoration adopted for the principal public rooms by Mr Arthur Davis of London, and Mr Benjamin W. Morris of New York, was in a 'restrained style suitable for a modern liner'. The 25 public rooms were elegant, displaying a refined dignity. However, the *Queen Mary* was not 'luxurious', nor was there 'unnecessary extravagance', while 'the opportunity has naturally been taken to incorporate the most modern improvements'. The launching of the *Queen Mary* after the

years of the Depression, was a great boost to British morale. On the other hand, Cunard had to tread a careful line between comfort and ostentation, the *moderne* style and the avant garde – they did not want to put customers off by being too outrageous. On several occasions interiors were toned down, despite the extra cost. In its own way the CUBE teapot underlined this by combining modernity with practicality. A CUBE price list of c1928 stated:

The modern tendency in everything is towards greater simplification of line and form in order to harmonise with the

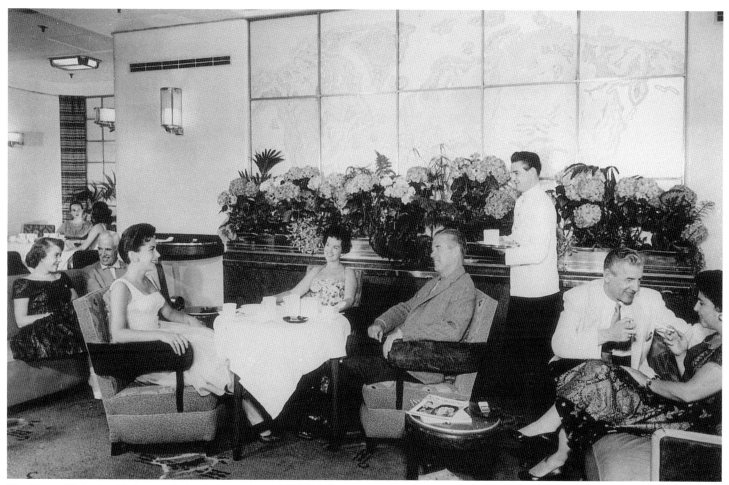

The Queen Elizabeth *cabin lounge with banded wares in use, 1950s/1960s. (Liverpool University)*

simplicity of modern architecture and decoration, at the same time aiming at economy in space.'

Of all the giant liners that crossed the Atlantic only the *Queen Mary* made a profit. The *Normandie*, probably the finest of them all, inhibited many potential passengers by her overwhelming luxury and she often sailed only half-full.

The CUBE obviously suited the new design ethos of the *Queen Mary*, and yet, remarkably, it was already nearly twenty years old. Bone china was supplied to the liner by Jackson & Gosling (the producers of Grosvenor China)

who had been supplying Cunard for the previous three years. George Clews of Tunstall supplied stoneware breakfast sets. Conventionally shaped cups were used with, as was noted by *The Shipbuilder,* 'unusually deep saucer wells', another feature dictated by experience.

CUBES were used in the cabin- or first-class and tourist- or second-class accommodation. For the *Queen Mary* the design was very simple, matching the dinner and breakfast crockery for the cabin and tourist classes, supplied by John Maddock & Sons, a firm which catered specially for ship and

The sitting room of a first-class suite on the Queen Elizabeth. *Note the VIP teaware with its gold print of 'lace-like delicacy' supplied by Plant. (Liverpool University)*

hotel requirements. The company supplied plates for meat, soup, salad (crescent-shaped), sweets and cheese, as well as hors-d'oeuvre dishes, consommé cups and stands (pedestal cup with a lobate stand), salad bowls, egg-cups, and breakfast cups and saucers, an aggregate of some 30,000 pieces. *The Shipbuilder*, which covered the entire fitting out of the *Queen Mary*, noted that the colour was a deep ivory, 'simply but tastefully relieved with bands of golden brown, grey and black'. This pattern was to be adopted by the other ships of the Cunard fleet, the *Queen Elizabeth* and the new *Mauretania*. Jackson & Gosling continued to provide tablewares after

1949, but were joined by E. Brain & Co. who supplied their Foley China. Pieces can be dated by their marks and during the period 1934-1949, marks include the legend, 'Cunard White Star Line'; after 1949, when it had acquired sufficient White Star stock to control its subsidiary, Cunard reverted to its original nomenclature, 'Cunard Steam-ship Company'. The inclusion of the hyphen in the mark is important for dating purposes, denoting the period after 1949.

The CUBE-shaped stoneware supplied by George Clews was used for morning tea and breakfasts served in the staterooms. It was finished in pale, matt oatmeal glaze, which

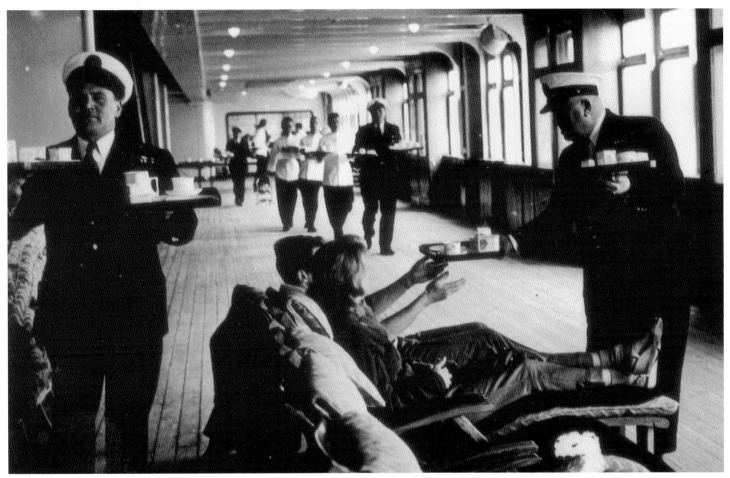

Passengers and staff aboard the Queen Elizabeth *or* Queen Mary, *from a series of promotional photographs. (Liverpool University)*

was supplied by the Phoenix Chemical Works, Hanley, owned by Harrison & Son. *The Pottery Gazette,* March 1936, considered this to be 'an achievement in the application of an artistic glaze to useful and inexpensive articles', while according to *The Shipbuilder,* it 'provides a happy illustration of the artistry which can enrich articles of everyday utility'. The reviewer in *The Pottery Gazette* was of the opinion that it was:

> perhaps a typical example of how articles of everyday utility are now being made in pleasing, as well as functional, form without loss of that simplicity which is characteristic of all really good design.

In addition, Clews supplied Souvenir ware, using a dark brown, shiny glaze. CUBE wares could be legitimately bought, so the honest passenger could take home a souvenir without a shadow of guilt and avoid difficulties at customs! A pure-white china coffee service was provided by Josiah Wedgwood & Sons Ltd., of Etruria, who were also responsible for ornamental 'flowerpots'. The table glass, some 20,000 pieces, was Stuart crystal, manufactured by Stuart & Sons, Ltd., of Stourbridge. Again the designs were understated with 'enrichment taking the form of circumferential bands, neatly cut in a design of contiguous segmental – clearly inspired by

The first-class smoking room on the second Mauretania, with no
sign of the earlier patterned ware used on the original
Mauretania. (Liverpool University)

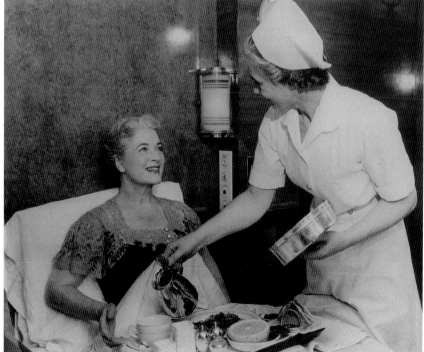

Breakfast with plain CUBES on the
second Mauretania, 1950s.
(Liverpool University)

the great ship's natural element.' All the china and glass was supplied by Stonier & Co., Ltd. of Liverpool. It is estimated that over 200,000 pieces of earthenware, china and glass were supplied for general ship's services, staterooms and bathrooms. Such suppliers held an important position, allowing a quick turnaround in port. By 1921 there were several well-known companies who supplied the shipping trade: Messrs T. and W. Ide, Ratcliffe, who supplied general glassware to the London-owned steamers, James Green and Nephew of London, and the Mercantile Stores Ltd. However, British manufacturers faced stiff competition from foreign companies, who were also keen to secure lucrative shipping contracts. Germany and Japan were offering good quality china at low prices. The cost of British china was high, as it was estimated that crockery lines were 'up' in price by 140% on an average with pre-war figures. Foreign companies also promised better delivery. The CUBE with its resistance to breakage and ease of storage would have given British manufacturers an edge over their foreign rivals.

The suppliers certainly needed large stocks – losses were evidently high, as it was quite 'a common thing' for stewards to 'chuck plates about for amusement'. Stonier's held stocks in the particular patterns required, so that when a ship docked they could replace the china within a day or two rather than wait for replacements to be made or delivered. Shipping companies could purchase direct, thereby saving costs but this necessitated warehouses at appropriate ports. Many were prepared to use 'seconds' to keep down costs. Consequently, collectors will often find pieces with imperfections. The vast quantities of china required, the need to keep down costs as breakages and losses were high, and the need for quick replacements, required the suppliers to place contracts with a number of firms. Stonier's, for example, had contracts with Minton's, Plant's and Copeland's for supplying the *Aquitania* and *Mauretania*. In essence, the ships got what was in stock and this accounts for the mixture of manufacturers and patterns on the earlier ships. With the launch of the *Queen Mary* the situation changed, as her livery was adopted by the rest of the Cunard fleet. This standardisation did not mean that only one manufacturer was used: contracts were placed with Jackson & Gosling and E. Brain for bone china and Sadler's was also used for the supply of plain, cream-coloured CUBES during the

1950s. These appear to have eventually superseded the oatmeal CUBES supplied by Clews. The examples illustrated in use on the *Queen Elizabeth* and new *Mauretania*, indicate that plain CUBE pieces were used for serving breakfast and tea in the cabins, alongside a metal thermos jug and banded earthenware pieces of the type supplied by Maddock & Son.

Stonier's, a firm dating back to the 1860s, had been supplying the shipping companies for many years. Their contract branches, with offices and warehouses, were at Bootle and Southampton and their main retail shop was in Lord Street, Liverpool, until 1941, when war damage forced a move into temporary accommodation in Williamson Square. In 1961 a new modern shop was built on this site. Stonier's also had retail premises in Southampton, Winchester and Southport. The company was founded by John Stonier, a Staffordshire man, who obviously recognised the potential of the transatlantic trade. He supplied one of the earliest passenger steamships, the SS *Great Britain*, launched in 1843 and the SS *Great Eastern*, launched in 1858. A notebook belonging to a commercial traveller, Thomas Hallett, lists an order on behalf of J. Stonier to Stuart & Sons, Ltd., for the *Great Eastern* dated January 1867. Fifteen years after founding the company, his fortune made, John Stonier retired. In 1876 he sold his business to Frederick Stuart, the well-known glass manufacturer from Edinburgh. Frederick's son, Arthur Stuart, and John Enoch Hawkins, formerly Stonier's manager, were put in charge. The name Stonier was retained and in 1880 Arthur Stuart and John Hawkins acquired full ownership. The company went on to equip such famous liners as the *Olympic*, the *Majestic* and the *Titanic*. In 1921 the contract department was separated from the main company and the branch in Southampton was opened. It was a standing joke against the firm that they increased their business by paying an honorarium to the pantry stewards for 'washing-up' the crockery by throwing it through the porthole'! Others observed that if the Atlantic were drained dry it would be possible to find one's way from Liverpool to New York by following the trail of Stonier's crockery. The last very large Cunard order was placed in 1968, when 143,000 pieces were supplied for the *Queen Elizabeth 2*. In 1997, Liverpool jewellers, David M. Robinson, bought Stonier's just as it was about to be closed down by its then owners, Waterford Crystal.

Tea on the Scythia *in the first-class enclosed garden lounge with patterned CUBES in use, including Plant's Tuscan China,* Bird of Paradise *pattern and Jackson & Gosling's Grosvenor China,* Rose *pattern, 1930s. (Liverpool University)*

For the *Queen Elizabeth*, which was to sail on the 10th March 1940, the same contractor, Stonier's of Liverpool, was used, and the same manufacturers. The orders for the *Queen Elizabeth* went in before the war but many of her fittings were not installed before the outbreak of hostilities and she sailed in 1946 as if for the first time. 150,000 pieces of British pottery and glass were commissioned, which must have been a boost to national morale. Indeed, the post-war slogan was 'Britain can make it!' Evidently made during the early days of

the war, the wares had since been stored away in safe places to avoid risks from bombing. The earthenware table service, of some 30,000 pieces, was supplied by John Maddock & Son, using the same design as that employed for the *Queen Mary*, a deep ivory colour simply decorated with bands of 'golden brown, grey and black'. The same company manufactured 30,000 pieces of tableware for the new *Mauretania*, supplied by Stonier's of Liverpool. Similarly, the matching china table service, also amounting to some 30,000 pieces, was supplied

Tea served on the deck of the second Caronia *– the 'Green Goddess'. (Liverpool University)*

by Copeland's Grosvenor works. The CUBE stoneware was supplied by George Clews and Co., in the pale matt oatmeal finish as used on the *Queen Mary*. R.H. & S.L. Plant also supplied a tea service with a burnished gold print of 'lace-like delicacy' in ivory china, and Wedgwood contributed a pure-white china coffee service, as well as jardinières for the floral decoration of the ship. It is interesting to note that Plant's, makers of Tuscan China, were still supplying the Cunard liners. They were one of the original suppliers of the CUBE

back in the late 1920s. However, the service they supplied for the *Queen Elizabeth* had a conventionally shaped teapot. According to some sources this service was reserved for VIPs and royal passengers, who were accorded the honour of a traditionally shaped pot. Such a service is certainly shown in use in the sitting room of a first-class suite. The example illustrated, with its long elegant spout, certainly suggests that the design would not have lasted for long in normal service.

Above, the tourist garden lounge on the Saxonia (1954) set with plain CUBES.

The new *Mauretania*, which sailed in 1939, also used the same contractors and designs, although early publicity material still showed the patterns used on the original *Mauretania*. George Clews supplied the stoneware CUBE sets in their, by now, distinctive matt oatmeal finish – 8,500 pieces were required for the new *Mauretania*. Tableware in the ivory banded pattern was again supplied by John Maddock & Sons, numbering some 30,000 pieces. Jackson & Gosling supplied the china CUBE services to match. R.H. & S. Plant, Josiah

Wedgwood and Royal Worcester were also suppliers, the latter for fireproof ware.

The *Queen Elizabeth 2*, which sailed in 1969, was still fitted with the CUBE, provided in plain off-white earthenware with gold banding – the CUBE shape was modified to produce a wider coffee pot. The pattern for the *QE2* was a very simple plain off-white body with gold banding and was produced by several firms including Myott & Sons and Fielding's, who produced Crown Devon ware. The CUBE was in use on the *QE2* until the 1980s, even though the CUBE Teapots Company had ceased to trade in 1968. It seems that the company used up their old stocks.

During the inter-war years the CUBE epitomised the *moderne* style. Not surprisingly it was chosen for the Cunard luxury liners where it graced the cabin- and tourist-class accommodation. The CUBE's compact shape was ideal for stowage. Its cubic design ensured stability and maximum safety at sea and the spoutless profile reduced breakages and conformed to new standards in hygiene. Its effectiveness is demonstrated by its length of service, from its first use on the *Mauretania* and *Aquitania* in the later 1920s until the 1980s on the *QE2*. The CUBE represented stylish modernity and practicality during the heyday of luxury liner living and perhaps it truly was the 'brilliant climax in teapot construction'.

EPILOGUE

The quest for the perfect teapot did not end with the CUBE. The cube shape was challenged, even at the height of its popularity, by streamlined forms. G.M. Creyke's T-FLO of 1937 and Clews' PERFECTO, available after the war, both adopted American streamlined styling. The 1950s saw the continuation, albeit often watered down, of 1930's modernist design. Tea drinking had been made simple by the arrival of the tea-bag rendering the strainer obsolete, but even the tea-bag has undergone major structural changes from square, to round and even pyramidal. More recently, there has been a revival of interest in the 'improved' pot, with advances like Bodum's glass teapot with infuser. This brings the story full circle, back to Green's HARROGATE patent infuser. Although the consumption of coffee has now overtaken tea, there is little doubt that the search will go on for the perfect teapot.

Advertisement from The Pottery Gazette, *1937.*

OTHER CUNARDERS WITH CUBE WARES
SCYTHIA (1921)

Scythia was the first of three 19,000 tonners built for Cunard to replace First World War losses. She was built for the passenger and cargo service to New York and could accommodate 337 first-, 331 second-, and 1,538 third-class passengers. In 1924 her second-class section was redesignated 'tourist class'. She largely sailed the route between Liverpool, Galway, Boston and New York, but she was also used for cruising. Perhaps the most notable features of the first-class section were the two garden lounges from which the passengers could watch the sea and storms in the security of glass-enclosed compartments. Sections of the promenade were also covered and enclosed. A garden lounge is illustrated, showing the CUBE wares in use. The patterns supplied were Plant's *Bird of Paradise* and Jackson & Gosling's *Rose*. After use in the war, she was reconditioned and back in service by August 1950. She was then used for the Quebec via Le Havre route, on which she was joined by the *Samaria*. She was taken out of service at the end of 1957.

Laconia (1922)

Sister ship to the *Scythia* and *Samaria*, and identical to them both internally and externally. The *Laconia* joined the transatlantic service in 1924, often sailing the route between Liverpool, Galway, Boston and New York. The patterns used were Plant's *Bird of Paradise* and Jackson & Gosling's *Rose*. These can be seen in the photograph of the covered and enclosed promenade. The *Laconia* was sunk in September 1942.

The 'A' Class of 1922
Andania, Ausonia and Antonia

A series of intermediate liners, all 13,000 tonners, were launched by Cunard for the London-Canada route. All three had accommodation for 500 first- and 1,200 third-class passengers. Essentially they were emigrant ships offering a one-way ticket for only £3. All three served in the war and never returned to civilian duties. Photographs show that, like the *Scythia* and *Laconia,* these ships had glass-enclosed garden rooms and a section of the promenades was also screened. The public rooms were small but comfortable. Dryad caneware furniture seems to have been used for seating. Both Plant's *Bird of Paradise* and Jackson & Gosling's *Rose* were used on these ships.

The 'A' Class of 1925
Aurania, Alaunia and Ascania

The second group of intermediate steamers launched by Cunard entered service in 1925. All three ships were 14,000 tonners and were similar in appearance to the earlier vessels of 1922. The *Aurania* was built for the New York service and the *Alaunia* and *Ascania* for the Canadian trade. They had accommodation for 400-500 cabin-class and approximately 1000 third-class passengers. While they could not rival the luxury of the big liners, the cabin-class public rooms were spacious and comfortable. Accommodation included a long gallery, drawing room, winter garden lounge, smoking room and gymnasium. The third-class passengers enjoyed a lounge and a smoking room. All three ships served in the war, but the only one to be returned to Cunard's service was the *Ascania*. She remained operational on the Liverpool to Montreal service until she was replaced by the new *Saxonia* and *Ivernia* in 1955. She was decommissioned the following year. An early photograph of the drawing room of the *Aurania* shows conventional teaware in use. A later photograph of the same interior shows both Plant's *Bird*

Patterned CUBES in use on the covered and enclosed promenade on the Laconia (1922), sister ship to the Scythia. (University of Liverpool)

The first-class sports-deck lounge on the Carinthia (1956), laid out with banded CUBES.

of *Paradise* and Jackson & Gosling's *Rose* simultaneously in use. The long gallery on the *Aurania* was decorated in a traditional style, effecting a Carolean look with mock late seventeenth-century panelling, gate-legged tables, chairs with barley-sugar twisted legs, and even leaded lights. The effect resembled the Carolean smoking room on the *Aquitania*, fitted in 1914.

Parthia (1947-48)

The *Parthia* was the sister ship of the *Media*. These two small vessels had the distinction of being the first passenger ships to enter service for Cunard in the post-war era. Both were just

over 13,000 tons and were good-looking ships with single funnels. They had accommodation for 250 passengers in one class. However, the passengers were well-catered for with six air-conditioned public rooms all situated on the promenade deck and a spacious sports deck. The most impressive area was the smoking room, whose large windows followed the curve of the bridge, allowing fine views. Due to competition from the airlines and industrial disputes these ships did not see long service. The *Parthia* was decommissioned in 1961. The illustration shows one of the

Tea on the Andania *(1922) with patterned CUBES and Dryad caneware furniture. (University of Liverpool)*

public rooms laid for tea. Perhaps surprisingly the CUBE service illustrated is Jackson & Gosling's *Rose*. In the post-war era one might expect to see the ivory banded design used on the *Queens* and the new *Mauretania*. The use of the older patterned china may be due to the setting up of publicity shots or the need to use existing supplies in the difficult years following the war. However, it is important to note that *Rose* patterned pieces with the later post-1949 Cunard mark have been found. Interestingly, the *Parthia* also used Moorcroft vases for the decoration of the lounge.

Caronia (1949)

The second *Caronia* can be described as the world's first purpose-built cruise ship and for twenty years after the Second World War she was extremely successful in this role. During her Cunard career her distinctive pale green livery earned her the nickname 'the Green Goddess'. The *Caronia* was renowned, particularly in the USA, for her world cruises. Due to her cruising role she had a yacht-like appearance with a single but enormous funnel midships. She was well-appointed with an open air lido and swimming

The drawing room on the Aurania (1925) with patterned CUBES in use, 1930s. (Liverpool University)

pool. The *Caronia* was a two-class ship with accommodation for 581 first- and 351 second-class passengers. Due to the length of the voyage, the cabins were large. Fares started at £52 for a second-class berth and went up to £82 for a first-class berth. She was launched by HRH Princess Elizabeth in October 1947 – the two restaurants, *Balmoral* and *Sandringham*, recalled this royal association. In January 1951, the *Caronia* left New York on the first of her legendary world

cruises. The itinerary took her to 30 ports, ranging from Mexico, the Pacific Islands and Australia to Malaya, India and the Mediterranean. There is no doubt that the *Caronia* earned much-needed dollars for the British economy during the austere years following the war. The bone china used on board was of the standard ivory banded type supplied by Jackson & Gosling, and Foley. Off-white earthenware CUBES were supplied by Sadler's.

The 1950s Quartet
Saxonia, Ivernia, Carinthia and Sylvania

At the close of the Second World War, Cunard had four ageing vessels of the 1920s on its Canadian service: the *Franconia, Ascania, Scythia* and *Samaria*. In 1951 it was decided to build a completely new class of ships for the Liverpool-Quebec-Montreal route. The first to go into service was the *Saxonia* in 1954. The last, the *Sylvania,* was not completed until 1957. By then the first jet aircraft, the Comet and Boeing 707, were nearing completion. The day of the transatlantic passenger ships was coming to an end.

As these ships were designed for the Canadian service, Canadian themes inspired much of the interior decoration such as Cartier's discovery of the St Lawrence River in 1536. The first-class cocktail bar of the *Saxonia* was decorated with Yukon themes, including the Beaver Dam Mural, while the first-class Maple Leaf Restaurant featured murals with the maple leaf and *fleur de lys* for the French connection, and the tomahawk and the bow and arrow to reflect native North American art. Heals Contracts Ltd., supplied much of the furniture, easy chairs, settees and upholstered stools. Ivory banded CUBE china was supplied for the first class, along with ivory banded dinner wares. The tourist garden lounge illustrates plain off-white CUBES, of the type supplied by Sadler's. In the first-class sports deck lounge of the *Carinthia* (1956), one can see the ivory banded pattern china in use.

Carmania (1954-1963)

This ship was in fact the renamed and reconditioned *Saxonia*. After difficult trading conditions, especially competition from the airlines, it was decided to give both the *Saxonia* and the *Ivernia* a fresh start. The *Ivernia* emerged from her refit for cruising as the *Franconia*. The contemporary furnishings and decor gave them the appearance of 'new ships'. The most striking feature was the large lido area with its kidney-shaped swimming pool and screened sun terrace. During the winter months both ships cruised from Florida to the Caribbean. As the illustration shows, the first-class lounge of the *Carmania* was modern and comfortable and ivory banded china CUBES still appear to be in use. Both the *Carmania* and the *Franconia* were sold by Cunard in 1973.

MANUFACTURERS OF THE CUBE
E. Brain & Co., Ltd.

Foley China Works, Fenton, Staffs (From 1903-1963)
Bone china. Makers of Foley China.
By 1904, E. Brain had acquired the Foley China Works in King Street, Fenton. Foley China was extremely good quality bearing printed marks incorporating the trade name 'Foley' or 'Foley China'. This was also used by Wileman & Co., which subsequently became 'Shelley' in 1925. Shelley never produced the CUBE, probably because of its rivalry with Foley China. Like Jackson & Gosling's 'Grosvenor China', Foley was popular among middle- and upper-class dealers, providing stylish decoration on a good body at a competitive price. Apparently, Brain's was the first company to produce the CUBE in bone china. Many talented artists and designers were associated with the firm which can be seen in the range of inventive designs used on CUBE shapes. CUBIST LANDSCAPE and CUBIST SUNFLOWER were introduced c1928. *The Pottery Gazette* noted that this firm was 'leaving no stone unturned' to bring out designs which were 'thoroughly appreciative of the trend of modern furnishing.' Foley's reputation was built on 'simplicity of style and dignified plainness of shape' – their house style was very distinctive. The vogue for bright colours had been followed, as seen in the CUBIST range and Foley was commended for its 'courageous handling' of designs. Several different patterns are illustrated, including one with an oriental flavour. Although some designs were daring, others were traditional, alien to the strict 'modernist' shape of the CUBE. In 1932, Thomas Acland Fennemore was appointed MD with the aim of improving the firm's commercial standing. He expanded the range of products and launched designs intended for mass distribution. In alliance with A.J. Wilkinson's Newport Pottery, the company engaged leading artists to design tableware. In 1934, work was shown at Harrod's in an Exhibition of Modern Art for the Table. which, although a critical success, was a commercial flop. After the war Foley supplied bone china CUBE shapes to the *Queen Mary*, the *Queen Elizabeth* and the new *Mauretania*, in what became the standard Cunard pattern for bone china: bands of brown, grey and black.
Buyers Notes, PG 1 October 1928
Karen McCready, *Art Deco and Modernist Ceramics* (London: Thames and Hudson) 1995, p139

George Clews and Co., Ltd.

Brownhills Pottery, Tunstall, Stoke-on-Trent (From 1906-61)
Earthenware and stoneware
Best known for the production of handpainted Chameleon Ware art pottery but Clews' mainstay was teapots. These were produced in a decorated pressed jet body, the red clay being dipped in a cobalt stained glaze which, upon firing, became a fine, jet-black. Ten years later, Samian red and Rockingham brown had largely replaced the jet. By 1919, Clews was 'A firm well known in the teapot trade'. The company manufactured the CUBE from c1925 and in 1936 supplied stoneware CUBE sets to Stonier's for the *Queen Mary* for morning tea and breakfasts served in the state rooms. They were glazed with either a pale matt oatmeal finish, or a shiny brown. The latter was used for Souvenir ware. The sets comprised teapot, coffee pot (lidded), hot-water jug, milk jug and sugar basin. Cups, saucers and plates were of standard shape. They also supplied the *Queen Elizabeth* with the same pale matt oatmeal finish. In 1939, the new *Mauretania* was equipped with 8,500 pieces of oatmeal CUBE ware. Such large orders must have been of great benefit to this small company. CUBE ware continued to be made at the Brownhills Pottery throughout the war, keeping the factory operational at a time when only undecorated ware was permitted to be made for the home market.

Clews also manufactured other patent teapots. The IXL or I excel (Patent No.327254), was a normal, round teapot with a small spout. This design had been patented by James and Thomas Clyde King in 1929. Their invention was a metal spout which was attached by means of a rubber washer to a hole in the front of a tea or coffee pot. They maintained that manufacturing costs would be reduced, as without a ceramic spout the teapots could be stacked more efficiently in the kiln. The user would benefit as the spout's sharp metal edge would instantly cut off any drip. The metal spout was removable for cleaning. Clews licenced this device from King, Sherrat and Lakin. The IXL automated advertisement, similar to the one used by the CUBE Teapots Company, toured china shops in the 1950s. It displayed a never-emptying teapot pouring into a never-overflowing cup. Post-war shortages restricted production, but in 1952 *The Pottery Gazette* noted 'a limited number of IXL non-drip teapots... are now being produced again by George Clews & Co., Ltd. following the recent shortage of metal spouts.'

The DUB-L-DEKR (DUBL-DEKR) was an ingenious design, composed of a teapot which fitted on top of a hot-water jug. Stacking pieces had been tried before but in this case the pot and jug appeared to form a whole, through the complementary shaping of the handles and spouts. Stacking obviously reduced cupboard space but, more importantly, the heat rising from the hot-water jug kept the tea hot. It was produced in at least two sizes, in matt oatmeal, yellow and green glazes and was probably introduced in the late 1930s. The oatmeal example illustrated bears the standard printed globe mark with 'made in England' dating to 1935+. Clews introduced their PERFECTO set at about the same time as the DUB-L-DEKR just before the start of World War Two. The PERFECTO set had teapot and water jug side-by-side on a matching pottery tray. The effect was reminiscent of the well-known Harold Stabler design put into production at Poole but the PERFECTO shapes were streamlined and can be compared with the T-FLO streamlined teapot, produced by G.M. Creyke from c1937. The PERFECTO set was produced for export after the war and features in one of Clews' rare advertisements in *The Pottery Gazette*, January 1947.

Hilary Calvert, *Chameleon Ware Art Pottery: A Collector's Guide to George Clews* (Atglen, USA: Schiffer Publishing Ltd), 1998

Copeland

Spode Works, Stoke-on-Trent (From 1847 to present day) In 1970 the company reverted to the old name of Spode in the form of Spode Ltd.
Bone china
It was Copeland's associated company, Jackson & Gosling, which produced the CUBE. From 1950 CUBES made for Cunard can be found marked Copeland's 'Grosvenor China'. In c1955, Copeland sold Jackson & Gosling to Thomas Poole who produced Royal Stafford China. However, Copeland supplied the Cunard Liners with a pattern, *Currents* (R4535) from c1914. The pieces seen date from 1914, 1924 and 1926. No CUBE shapes have been found. Copeland also supplied the White Star Line and Canadian Pacific Steamships Ltd., or CPS.

S. Fielding & Co., Ltd.

Railway Pottery, Devon Pottery (From 1911 onwards) Stoke-on-Trent

Earthenware. Makers of Crown Devon Ware.

Fielding's supplied the *QE2* which sailed in 1969, with CUBE shapes. The coffee pot was adapted and made wider. The pattern was a very simple off-white with gold banding around the rims. Pieces are marked with the standard Crown Devon mark, in use from c1930, normally in gold. Myott was also a *QE2* supplier.

Gibson & Sons, Ltd.

Albany Pottery, Harvey and Chelsea Potteries, Burslem, Stoke-on-Trent (From 1885 to 1985)

Earthenware

Allegedly, the largest teapot specialists in the trade. The WEMBLEY spoutless teapot was launched in 1922 and modified in 1923 into a more obviously cubic shape. CAP-ALL was introduced in 1929. The firm produced a wide variety of types, from plain Rockingham and Jet to unique designs in rich ground colours with gold finishes. Gibson made the CUBE from c1925 in many different finishes and stated 'there are scores of equally attractive decorations to be had upon the same shape.' Gibson supplied the Commonwealth and Dominion Line (1914-1937), later the Port Line (1937-1981), with CUBE teapots in the *Cornflower* pattern (PN6034) in which both CUBE and normal shapes were supplied. In addition to the Gibson mark they carry a Hammersley backstamp.

Buyers Notes, PG 1 October 1925
Buyers Notes, PG 1 February 1929

Grimwades Ltd.

Winton, Upper Hanley and Elgin Potteries, Stoke-on-Trent (From 1900)

Earthenware and Bone china. Producers of 'Royal Winton'.

This company supplied the Leicester showrooms of the CUBE Teapots Company. A wide variety of patterns and finishes was offered. Several of these are illustrated. Some of the more traditional patterns offered compromised the 'modernist' severity of the CUBE.

T.G. Green & Co., Ltd.

Church Gresley, nr Burton-on-Trent, Derby (From 1864 to the present day)

Earthenware and stoneware

Today, T.G. Green is best known for Cornish Ware. However, the factory also took an interest in improved teapots, being one of the first firms to invent a non-drip spout, the ACME, introduced in 1899 and still in use in 1922; by c1915 they were also marketing their HARROGATE INFUSER. As one of the suppliers for the CUBE Teapots Company's headquarters and showrooms in Leicester, Green's played a significant role in the story of the CUBE. They supplied the CUBE in a wide range of patterns and plain finishes, some of which are illustrated. They also produced the CUBE Compact Teaware, including the palette and cup.

Buyers Notes, PG 1 April 1922

Hammersley & Co.

Staffordshire Potteries, Longton, Staffs (Hammersley & Co. operated from c1887 to 1932, when it was retitled Hammersley & Co. (Longton Ltd.) from 1932-1974. In 1970 the firm was taken over by Copeland and retitled Hammersley China Ltd. in 1974)

Bone china

Although not mentioned as manufacturers of the CUBE in either the 1925 or 1928 advertisement, this company certainly produced the famous teapot and examples are illustrated. In addition, the Hammersley backstamp has been found in conjunction with Gibson & Sons, Ltd., on CUBES for the Commonwealth and Dominion Line (1914-1937), later the Port Line (1937-1981). Presumably Hammersley were responsible for adding the printed *Cornflower* pattern (PN6034).

Jackson & Gosling Ltd.

Grosvenor Works, Longton, Stoke-on-Trent, Staffs (From 1866, Longton address from 1909)

Associated with Copeland from 1932, when Arthur Hewitt of Jackson & Gosling joined the board of W.T. Copeland when it became a limited company. The standard mark became Copeland's 'Grosvenor China, England' but ceased in the mid-

1950s when Copeland sold the firm to Royal Stafford China. Bone China. Makers of 'Grosvenor China'.

Grosvenor China was a popular line amongst the middle and upper classes, providing stylish decoration on a good body at a competitive price. Shapes and patterns tended to be traditional. An advertisement in *Good Housekeeping*, 1928, was designed to promote their 'exclusive *period* designs'. The Grosvenor range of Old English Teasets sold from 3 to 25 guineas. A full range of useful table articles was offered for the English, Colonial and American markets. In 1938 the company, now an associated firm of W.T. Copeland & Sons, was still offering a good, middle-grade brand of china. Even at this date, the firm still specialised in its Old English decorations: 'they have a whole range of excellent designs in the antique spirit.' However, they also offered 'decorations of modern impulse' and did a good trade in badged wares. By 1920 the pattern numbers had reached 5500. The company began producing the CUBE from c1928 and started supplying Cunard in c1933. Patterns include *Rose* which was also made in Foley Bone China after the war. Jackson & Gosling supplied bone china CUBE shapes to the *Queen Mary*, the *Queen Elizabeth* and the new *Mauretania* in what became the standard Cunard pattern for bone china – bands of brown, grey and black. E. Brain, Foley China, supplied this pattern in the 1950s and also produced CUBE wares for general trade. The example illustrated has a bold, colourful, handpainted pattern, somewhat reminiscent of Clarice Cliff.

Buyers Notes, PG September 1920
Buyers Notes, PG June 1938

Alfred B. Jones & Sons Ltd.

Grafton Works, Longton, Staffordshire (From 1880-1972. From 1968-1972 the company was owned by Crown House. In 1972, the name was changed to Royal Grafton Bone China Crown Lynn Ceramics (UK) Ltd.)

Bone china. Producers of Grafton China or Royal Grafton. First mentioned as a CUBE manufacturer in the advertisement for 1928.

Minton Ltd.

Stoke-on-Trent, Staffordshire (Established 1793 to the present day)

Earthenware and Bone china

Minton's supplied the Cunard Liners *Mauretania* and *Aquitania* with CUBE shapes from the late 1920s. Standard patterns include *Cuckoo* and *Indian Tree*. Care should be taken not to confuse these patterns with Plant's Tuscan China *Bird of Paradise*, or Copeland's *Currents* (R4535). All the pieces carry the pre-1934 Cunard mark. In addition, Minton's supplied Lyons Corner Houses with the same patterns.

Myott, Son & Co., Ltd.

Cobridge (1902-46) and Hanley, Staffordshire (c1947) (From 1898 to the present day)

Earthenware

Myott supplied the *QE2* which sailed in 1969, with CUBE shapes. The coffee pot was adapted and made wider. The pattern was a very simple off-white with gold banding around the rim. Fielding's Crown Devon was also a *QE2* supplier.

R.H. & S.L. Plant Ltd.

Longton, Staffordshire. (From c1898 to the present day.)

Bone China. Makers of Tuscan China.

This firm operated the Tuscan Works, Forester Street, Longton, producing a good range of useful and decorative wares. The partnership was formed into a limited company in 1915. Marks normally include the trade name Tuscan China. Pattern 5728H had been reached by 1937. In 1966 the firm became part of the Wedgwood group. Plant supplied their Tuscan China to the Cunard Line after the First World War. CUBE shapes were introduced c1926-28. *Bird of Paradise*, PN9030 and 9033, was supplied to the *Mauretania* and *Aquitania*. Souvenir pieces in this pattern were also produced. Beware of the similarity of this pattern to Minton's *Cuckoo* and Copeland's *Currents*, also in use on the same ships.

James Sadler and Son Ltd.

Wellington and Central Potteries, Burslem, Stoke-on-Trent, Staffs (From c1899 to the present day)

Earthenware, mainly teapots. Also manufactured the PINE LOCK-LID teapot, the NESTA range, the HANDY HEXAGON and the CAFE shape and the EVERCLEAN Patent Hygenic Teapot.

Sadler's are best known for their novelty teapots, including their famous motor car produced in the 1930s. For the café and restaurant trade they produced several 'useful' lines from plain or roughened russet with sunken lids and stubby spouts to 'unique' decorated pots in the spoutless HANDY HEXAGON shape. In 1938, 'Buyer's Notes' in *The Pottery Gazette* featured Sadler's new Soccer teapot, the handle formed by a footballer throwing the ball from the touchline. The spout resembled the referee's whistle. By that time there was a great demand for handpainted decoration on ivory and matt glazes rather than the glossy varieties. By 1936 the firm had installed a modern continuous tunnel oven, allowing greater volume and even firing, obviating the risks of crazing. At the 1936 British Industries Fair, Sadler's offered a wide range of articles for use in cafés and hotels, including their famous 'roughed ware' and, a new addition, the EVERCLEAN. During the 1950s, Sadler's became a major Cunard supplier. A variety of patterns have been found including a plain off-white or cream, small pink rosebuds, green stars, blue stars, and a bold red and black abstract design. Only the plain off-white pieces are definitely for Cunard's. The patterns may have been added by Sadler's to pieces with the Cunard backstamp but not intended for use on the ships. These pieces were all supplied by Stonier's of Liverpool.

Buyers Notes, *PG* February 1931
Buyers Notes, *PG* February 1936
Buyers Notes, *PG* May 1938

Wedgwood and Co., Ltd.

Unicorn and Pinnox Works, Tunstall, Staffordshire (From c1860 to the present day)
Earthenware
This Tunstall company should not be confused with the Josiah Wedgwood firm, although it is now part of the Wedgwood group of companies. Wedgwood is listed as manufacturer in both the 1925 and 1928 advertisements.

Arthur Wood

Bradwell Works, Longport, Staffordshire. (From 1904 to 1928. Continued as Arthur Wood and Son (Longport) Ltd., Staffs, from 1928 to present day)
Earthenware
Specialist in teapots and teasets, hot-water jugs, coffee and cocoa jugs, sugars and creams and sets of jugs. Produced in a wide range of finishes including Samian, Rockingham, Russet and self-coloured glazes, silver and gold lustres and Derby-style Imari patterns. The first company to manufacture a ceramic CUBE in 1920. Arthur Wood was included in the list of manufacturers in the 1925 advertisement announcing the CUBE Teapots Company. An advertisement dated 1928, gives the new nomenclature, Arthur Wood and Son. This indicates that Wood's were manufacturing the CAMEL non-drip teapot.

Buyers Notes, *PG* February 1936
Buyers Notes, *PG* February 1936

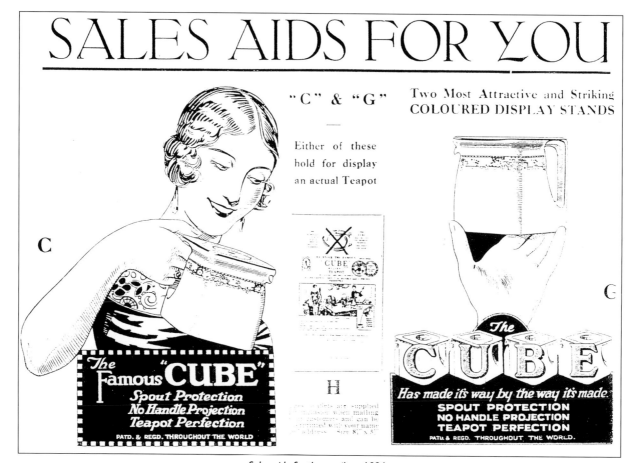

Sales aids for the retailer, c1926.

Left, CUBE Teapots Ltd., reverse of promotional postcard shown in colour on page 38, c1926-32, featuring the CUBE Early Morning Teaset in primrose yellow.

MARKS

Arthur Wood,
c1920-25

Cube Teapots Co., Ltd.
often found without
manufacturer's mark

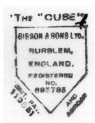

Gibson & Sons, from
1925

Elkington plate,
Elkington & Co.,
from c1925

Silver plate by T.
Wilkinson & Sons,
from c1925

Grimwades Ltd., from
1926

Foley China, from
1926

Jackson & Gosling, pre-
1934

Tuscan China for the
Cunard Line, pre-
1934

Brain's Foley China,
1934-49

George Clews & Co.,
Ltd. for the Cunard
Line, c1936

Sadler & Sons, from
1949

Crown Devon, from
1969

Myott, from 1969

BIBLIOGRAPHY

General/Ceramic

Calvert, Hilary, *Chameleon Ware Art Pottery: A Collector's Guide to George Clews*, (Atglen USA: Schiffer Publishing Ltd), 1998

Elliot, Malcolm, 'The Leicester Coffee-House and Cocoa Movement', reprinted from the *Trans. of the Leicestershire Archaeological and Historical Society*, Vol.XLVII, 1971-2

Godden, Geoffrey, *Encyclopaedia of British Pottery and Porcelain Marks*, (London: Barrie and Jenkins), 1964, (reprinted 1900)

McCready, Karen, *Art Deco and Modernist Ceramics* (London: Thames and Hudson), 1995

Meldrum, Rose, 'The Cube Teapot', *Newsletter of the Northern Ceramics Society*, 1985, Vol.60, p26)

Cunard and Shipping

A Special Correspondent, 'Liverpool and the New *Mauretania*: Equipment Sidelight: Ceramic and Glass Supplies, *The Pottery and Glass Record*, July 1939, pp177-180

Akers, John B. (ed), *From the Cradle to the Sea: A biographical study of the RM Queen Mary Maiden Voyage, Southampton, Cherbourg and New York, May 27th, 1936* Glasgow: Cunard/White Star Liner), March 1936, p14

Anon., 'Pottery, Tiles and Glass on Modern Liners: Shipping Companies as Promoters of Taste', *The Pottery and Glass Record*, 1925, pp411-415

Anon., 'Pottery and Glass Distribution in Liverpool: A famous distributing house and an historic shipping contract', *The Pottery Gazette*, 2 March 1936, p400

Anon., 'The Queen Mary', *The Shipbuilder and Marine Engine-Builder*, June 1936, p184

Anon., 'The Queen Elizabeth', *The Pottery Gazette and Glass Trade Review*, December 1946, p802

Anon., 'Stonier's, Stuart and Ship's Supplies', *The Pottery Gazette and Glass Trade Review* (incorporating *Tableware*), May 1969, p449

Anon., 'The Cunard White Star RMS Queen Mary: A notable shipping achievement', *The Pottery and Glass Record*, September 1936, pp226-231

'Exporter, Supplies for the Steamship Companies', *The Pottery and Glass Record*, June 1921, pp287-88

Haws, Duncan, *Cunard Line*, Merchant Fleet Series Vol.12 (Burwash, East Sussex: Travel Creatours Ltd or TCL), 1990

Haws, Duncan, *Port Line with Corry, Royden, Tyser and Milburn*, Merchant Fleet Series 21 (Hereford: TCL), 1990

Haws, Duncan, *The Burma Boats: Henderson and Bibby*, Merchant Fleet Series 29 (Hereford: TCL), 1996

Hyde, Francis E., *Cunard and the North Atlantic 1840-1973: A History of Shipping and Financial Management*, (London and Basingstoke: Macmillan Press), 1975

Krummes, Daniel C., *Dining on Inland Seas: Nautical China from the Great Lakes Region of North America*, (Michigan: Nautical Works Press), 1997

Outwater, Myra Yelin, *Ocean Liner Collectables*, (Atglen, USA: Schiffer Books), 1998

Watson, Nigel, *The Bibby Line 1807-1900: A Story of Wars, Booms and Slumps*, (London: James and James, Landscape Books), 1990